LINES OF ARGUMENT

FOR VALUE DEBATE

LINES OF ARGUMENT
FOR VALUE DEBATE

CAROL WINKLER

Georgia State University

WILLIAM NEWNAM

Emory University

DAVID BIRDSELL

City University of New York, Baruch College

WCB Brown &
Benchmark
P U B L I S H E R S

Madison, Wisconsin•Dubuque, Iowa•Indianapolis, Indiana
Melbourne, Australia•Oxford, England

Book Team

Editor *Stan Stoga*
Developmental Editor *Mary E. Rossa*
Production Editor *Jayne Klein*
Visuals/Design Developmental Consultant *Marilyn A. Phelps*
Visuals/Design Freelance Specialist *Mary L. Christianson*
Publishing Services Specialist *Sherry Padden*
Marketing Manager *Carla J. Aspelmeier*
Advertising Manager *Jodi Rymer*

Brown & Benchmark

A Division of Wm. C. Brown Communications, Inc.

Vice President and General Manager *Thomas E. Doran*
Editor in Chief *Edgar J. Laube*
Executive Editor *Ed Bartell*
Executive Editor *Stan Stoga*
National Sales Manager *Eric Ziegler*
Director of CourseResource *Kathy Law Laube*
Director of CourseSystems *Chris Rogers*
Director of Marketing *Sue Simon*
Director of Production *Vickie Putman Caughron*
Imaging Group Manager *Chuck Carpenter*
Manager of Visuals and Design *Faye M. Schilling*
Design Manager *Jac Tilton*
Art Manager *Janice Roerig*
Permissions/Records Manager *Connie Allendorf*

Wm. C. Brown Communications, Inc.

President and Chief Executive Officer *G. Franklin Lewis*
Corporate Vice President, President of WCB Manufacturing *Roger Meyer*
Vice President and Chief Financial Officer *Robert Chesterman*

Cover and interior design by Carol S. Joslin

Copyedited by Jeff Putnam

A Times Mirror Company

Library of Congress Catalog Card Number: 92–71745

ISBN 0–697–13241–2

Printed in the United States of America by Wm. C. Brown Communications, Inc.,
2460 Kerper Boulevard, Dubuque, IA 52001

10 9 8 7 6 5 4 3 2 1

Contents

viii   **Contents**

Preface

Lines of Argument for Value Debate is part of a three-part instructional series about argumentation and debate. It is designed to be used in conjunction with *Lines of Argument,* a core text which introduces the topical traditions of argumentation as they apply to general debate issues of research, evidence, reasoning, delivery, cross-examination, flowcharting, and ethics. This companion text supplements the core volume by identifying the lines of argument specific to value debate.

Lines of Argument for Value Debate differs from most textbooks on the debate market. Rather than treat all of the stock issues in a single chapter as the components of a prima facie case, it devotes a full chapter to each of the general lines of argument in value debate. Chapter Four, for example, explores the issue of justification in value debates. The chapter begins by identifying the lines of argument useful for establishing justification for the value resolution, continues with lines of argument useful for denying the justification of the resolution, and ends with the lines of argument that help debaters resolve conflicting claims of justification.

To help beginning debaters understand the far-reaching applicability of the general lines of argument in value debate, we provide a variety of examples. In most of the chapters, a running argument between two characters illustrates each of the argumentative options. We also provide excerpts from the Cross-Examination Debate Association Tournament Championship Rounds so that beginning debaters can understand how the lines of argument appear in actual intercollegiate debates. While these debates are useful examples of conventional competitive practices, instructors may wish to warn their students that the examples frequently lack complete citation of evidence. Some minor editing of the final round transcripts made the sample arguments more accessible and more easily understood by beginning debaters. The authors would like to thank Jim Brey, Director of Forensics at Florida State University, for his willingness to grant permission to use the excerpts of the debates.

While each of the general lines of argument are considered independently, the Value text also includes a chapter that explores the interrelationships between the various arguments in a debate. By showing debaters ways to use argumentative interrelationships to minimize their opponent's arguments and maximize their own, the book develops a more integrated perspective about the multitude of arguments that can occur in a single context.

Having armed the debater with the material to begin to debate, the Value text shifts to a discussion of the form of contemporary debate. Chapter Six explores the types of arguments that conventionally occur in each of the constructive and rebuttal speeches. Goals are established for each speech in team debate and Lincoln-Douglas formats. Throughout the chapter, we use a single hypothetical debate to illustrate what each speaker is expected to do.

The Value text concludes by considering how the lines of argument interact with different perspectives on debate evaluation. Prominent debate paradigms are presented. Instructors using this text should feel free to use those portions of the text that are relevant for the skill and experience level of their debaters. As an introductory text, *Lines of Argument for Value Debate* starts at the beginning, introducing the basics of the activity. It does not, however, stop with traditional introductory considerations; it explores the multiplicity of options available for arguing a point. As a result, some sections may not be appropriate for every classroom. To facilitate "editing" of this sort, the text has been designed to accommodate instructors who may want to drop some of the more complex material. No basic discussions in any chapter depend on the advanced discussions in some other chapter.

As an example, examine Chapter Two, "Analyzing Topicality Through Lines of Argument." The early portions of the chapter, the identification of key terms and sources of definition, are relevant to all beginning debaters. However, the section on standards for evaluating competing definitions may be too extensive for the average debate class. This section might be more useful to debaters who plan to participate in interscholastic debate tournaments. Instructors should not hesitate to eliminate such a section from their reading lists. The lines of argument approach presents argumentative options for debaters; beginners can use the earlier material without reading the later material. Advanced students can benefit from both sections.

One of our primary goals for writing *Lines of Argument for Value Debate* was to remove much of the mystery that surrounds competitive debate. By relying on the general topics of value debate, we hope that we have provided access to many students who might have been intimidated by an activity that seems exclusively for the elite. Debaters at all levels should find options for value argument in this book that they may never have considered or examined in a systematic way.

Acknowledgements

Since beginning work on this book we have benefited from the wisdom of a great many colleagues working in the field of debate and argumentation. We are particularly thankful for the careful and insightful criticism from the review teams assembled by Brown & Benchmark: Steven R. Brydon, California State University, Chico; Nicolas Burnett, California State University, Sacramento; Alan Cirlin, St. Mary's University; Joseph M. Corcoran, California State University, Chico; Dale Hample, Western Illinois University; William Keith, University of Louisville; Michael Leigh, Orange Coast College; Edward L. Schiappa, Purdue University; and Paul Scovell, Salisbury State College. In addition, Melissa Wade and Kathleen Hansel of Emory University and Judy Butler of Spelman College provided advice and encouragement. Together, these critics challenged us to write a much better book than we could have on our own; errors that remain are no fault of theirs.

We would like to thank Georgia State University, Emory University, and Baruch College for providing us with the necessary support to complete this project. In particular, the authors would like to thank Marsha Stanback for providing grant support for the project in her role as chairperson of the Communications Department at Georgia State. Kimberly Kline devoted numerous hours of necessary computer assistance. Greg Huber of Emory provided much needed assistance with graphics. We would also like to thank Jim Brey of Florida State University for allowing us to use transcripts of championship debates.

The staff at Brown & Benchmark have made authorship of a three-volume text as uncomplicated as the task can be. Special thanks are due Stan Stoga, an editor who encouraged the project and strived to improve it from its original conception. Thanks also to copy editors Martha Morss and Jeff Putnam, who did wonders for our prose.

We owe a great deal to the faculty of the National High School Institute of Speech. The collegial atmosphere of Northwestern University's institute produced a body of debate knowledge that surfaces throughout this three-book series. Many of the ideas in this text were shaped by the outstanding teachers who have worked in that program. We would like to thank David Zarefsky, Erwin Chimerensky, and Edward Schiappa, all directors of the institute, for providing a rich and rewarding environment in which to explore the debate process.

Finally, we would like to thank friends and family for their understanding during a lengthy process. Jean Gallagher was kind and tolerant and even paused to rework some of the more infelicitous language.

1

The Nature of Value Debate

Chapter Outline

Process of Value Debate
General Lines of Argument and Value Debate
Summary and Conclusions

Key Terms

resolutions
topical
topicality
criteria
justification
burden of proof
presumption
affirmative
negative
constructive
rebuttal
case
off-case
judge

Monte: Household chores aren't fair around here. I've been taking out the garbage ever since I can remember just because I'm male. I get the dirty, cold, unpleasant job while Mindy gets to do light household work. The only fair way would be to rotate chores.

Sonya: Professors Learnalot and Bookworm both want me to write papers on the Great Depression. I can't see developing different topics for each class. The honor code says that it's wrong to substitute previously prepared papers for new work. But this paper would be entirely new; I'd just turn it in twice. I want to follow the honor code, but it isn't clear, and I can't believe that it requires senseless work.

Dean Dollar: We have a choice between two dreadful options: our school must either raise tuition or cut enrollment. Because the university has an obligation to the students of this state to let any qualified applicant attend, we must choose the former. Without the financial support of a tuition increase, we will have to reduce course offerings in all areas. A tuition hike will make it harder for lower-income students to attend, but failure to generate revenue will make it impossible for many more students—rich and poor alike—to come to class at all.

What kind of arguments are Monte, Sonya, and Dean Dollar making? It would be easy to say that they bear no relationship to one another, ranging as they do from a child's arguments over chores to an administrator's arguments about university policy. The issues are undoubtedly quite different from one another, but take another look. There are considerable similarities in the *kinds* of arguments being made.

To begin with, each speaker defends a more or less explicit statement of value. In your core text accompanying this value supplement, we noted that such explicit statements of value are called **resolutions** in academic debate. If we were to reformulate their positions along the resolutional guidelines discussed in your core text, they might look something like the following:

Monte—Resolved: that chore rotation is more desirable than assigning chores by gender.
Sonya—Resolved: that submitting the same paper twice is justified.
Dean Dollar—Resolved: that ensuring course offerings is more important than providing a low tuition.

Each of these resolutions addresses an issue of value, therefore, this form of debating is referred to as value debate. We use the term *value* in many contexts in our lives. We can value bicycles because they are beautiful or because they are useful. We can value friends because they are honorable or fair. We understand values as concepts such as beauty, honesty, and fairness. Because the term is broad, we define values as the expressions of the worth of a person, process, thing, or idea.

Sometimes we are forced to choose between values. Suppose that your best friend were to say that you could not continue to be friends unless you surrendered your bicycle to him or her. Now you have a conflict. Knowing both the bicycle and the friendship have value will not help to determine which has more importance. You need additional conceptual tools to resolve such conflicts.

One of the first steps in resolving conflicting claims of value is to establish the meaning of the resolution. Monte, Sonya, and Dean Dollar all attempt to define the values that they advocate. Monte defines desirable in terms of the fairness in rotation of chores that prevents him from always being stuck doing a "dirty, cold, unpleasant" job. Sonya limits her definition of justified academic conduct to work that makes sense. She cannot believe that the honor code would require her to do "senseless" work. Dean Dollar is trying to define the educational mission of the school. If the Board of Regents accepts the dean's definition of budget constraints and the school's educational mission, they may very well decide to raise tuition. In any debate over values, advocates must define the terms of the debate to identify relevant arguments. If the arguments presented by the affirmative fall within the scope of the resolution, the affirmative is considered to be **topical.** Value debaters call arguments over the definition of terms **topicality.**

Monte, Sonya, and Dean Dollar also establish criteria for determining that their values should be affirmed. Monte tries to convince his parents that fairness should be the criterion for determining household duties. Sonya tries to convince herself that the school honor code should determine what value to uphold. Dean Dollar thinks that the educational mission of the university should determine whether to increase tuition. Each advocate attempts to establish a method for evaluating the probable truth of the value resolution. **Criteria** arguments establish a method for evaluating the probable truth of a value resolution.

Monte, Sonya, and Dean Dollar also argue that the values they support are relevant to their respective situations. Monte argues that he has taken out the garbage ever since he could remember, while Mindy has performed less difficult chores. Fairness would dictate that Mindy should take out the garbage for a while. Sonya argues that the honor code does not address the issue of writing the same paper for two classes. Because the honor code does not mention it and she will be able to spend more time on her other classes, Sonya feels justified writing only one paper. Dean Dollar can argue that raising tuition is the best way to serve as many students as possible. Under this standard, the school better serves its mission by raising tuition rather than cutting programs. The advocates justify the values they support according to the criteria they establish. **Justification** arguments are illustrations of the practical significance of a value argument.

As you can see, even though Monte, Sonya, and the dean are presenting very different cases, they cover the same kinds of arguments. These arguments will recur in any developed dispute over values. Advocates of value resolutions have to define what they mean by the resolution, establish a method of assessing the probable truth of the claim, and justify affirming the resolution, in the context of the debate. Taken together, these types of arguments constitute the affirmative **burden of proof:** the requirement that those affirming values must demonstrate topicality, criteria, and justification.

Typically, when discussing any statement of value, we hold the person who advances that statement responsible for proving it worthy of our support. The assumption that the value resolution is probably untrue until proven otherwise is referred to as **presumption.** Presumption places the burden of proof on those who advocate the values in the resolution. Presumption is the reason why affirmative debaters—who always defend the resolution—are charged with the burden of proof.

Monte, Sonya, and Dean Dollar can overcome presumption against the resolutions they defend by fulfilling the burden of proof regarding definition, criteria, and justification. When Monte, Sonya, and the dean convince, respectively, Monte's parents, Sonya's conscience, and the Board of Regents that an important value decision is necessary, that appropriate criteria exist to evaluate the conflict, and that affirming the value is justified, they will overcome the presumption against their positions.

Monte, Sonya, and the dean introduced us to the fundamental concepts that recur in value debate. Formal academic debate shares these general lines of argument with informal discussions, such as those about garbage and term paper procedures. Unlike informal arguments, however, academic debate has several important conventions to help ensure education and competitive fairness.

Process of Value Debate

Academic debates involve two competing sides: an **affirmative** side, charged with defending the formal debate resolution, and a **negative** side, charged with denying the resolution. In most debates, the sides comprise two individuals, or a team. Each debater offers a **constructive** speech where they establish new arguments and issues in support of this position, and a **rebuttal** speech where they resolve and summarize the previous arguments presented in the debate. The speeches are timed to ensure that both sides have equal time to defend their positions.

The affirmative side in value debate must identify the value they support, a criteria for evaluating the resolution, and a justification for affirming the resolution. These arguments provide a rationale for the resolution and they are referred to under the collective title of the **case** arguments. The negative side in the debate may attack any or all of the case arguments. In addition, the negative side may elect to defend competing values which they find to be more important than those affirmed in the resolution. These negative arguments are usually referred to as the **off-case** arguments.

Unlike informal discussions, formal debate places a great importance on the use of evidence and well-developed arguments. Debaters are expected to support their positions with evidence since very few students are experts in the subject matters of competitive debate. While evidence is necessary, it is not sufficient to win debates. Opponents can identify flaws in your evidence. All arguments are subject to attack and both sides are prepared to debate. Therefore, it is very important that you prepare sound arguments supported by strong evidence. Like library research, these positions should be carefully prepared and critiqued prior to an actual debate round.

A **judge** decides which side wins the debate. The judge evaluates the arguments in support of the affirmative case and compares those arguments with the arguments that deny the resolution. Based on the standards established in the debate, the judge votes for the affirmative or negative side.

General Lines of Argument and Value Debate

Value debates, then, include arguments that are predictable. This is fortunate for debaters because they can identify the recurrent arguments and be better prepared when they engage in an actual debate. In Chapter Two of the core text we identified two types of arguments: general and specific. General lines of argument will be present regardless of the subject. In the field of value debate, those lines of argument are: that a value is clearly defined, that appropriate criteria exist to evaluate the resolution, and that the value in the resolution is justified. Specific lines of argument, on the other hand, are dependent on the subject area under discussion. The reasons why Monte values fairness in household duties, for example, may be completely irrelevant to the dean's interest in tuition increases.

We devote the remainder of this text to introducing you in more detail to the general lines of argument that recur in value debate. We use specific lines of argument that might occur in particular subject areas to illustrate how the lines of argument function. We focus each of the next three chapters of the book (Chapters Two through Four) on the general lines of argument in value debate. We analyze each argument separately to identify further lines of argument that affirm topicality, criteria, and justification. Each chapter then analyzes lines of argument to negate topicality, criteria, and justification. Finally, we indicate the arguments useful in resolving conflicts between the two.

This introduction to the general lines of argument in value debate should prepare you to succeed in the specific circumstances of any value debate. By applying the general lines of argument to the particulars of an argumentative situation, you will be able to generate specific lines of argument for specific resolutions.

We analyze each line of argument separately in each chapter. Do not, however, be misled into thinking that you can treat them separately in a debate. We analyze the lines of argument independently so that you will understand these arguments in depth, but the three lines of argument are connected and interdependent. Remember that the affirmative debater must overcome presumption against the resolution by proving that the value affirmed is topical, can be assessed appropriately, and is justified by that assessment. These arguments need to be learned in detail, but only *together* do they form a complete rationale for the resolution. The individual arguments are important, but so are the interrelationships between them.

In Chapter Five we pay particular attention to the interaction among the three general lines of argument. We offer debaters an analytical view of the strategic opportunities they may discover in an academic debate. Understanding interrelationships among arguments allows you to develop complete and coherent arguments of your own. Knowing how arguments interact also provides you with an opportunity to identify the inconsistencies and irrelevancies of your opponents' arguments.

In Chapter Six we present the traditional roles of each speaker in the debate. We examine the conventional application of the three general lines of argument in an academic debate. We identify standard time limits, orders of speeches, and the formal expectations debaters should anticipate.

In Chapter Seven we explore how debate judges evaluate the general lines of argument in debate. We explain the different perspectives judges may bring into a debate. We also examine the potential biases of judges and provide guidance for identifying such biases. Through this process, we suggest ways to appeal to judges.

Summary and Conclusions

To be effective value advocates, debaters must understand that three general lines of arguments recur in every value debate. These include clearly defining the resolution, establishing appropriate criteria to assess the value resolution, and justifying the value resolution in a particular context.

In value debates, an affirmative side charged with defending the resolution and a negative side attempting to deny the resolution each try to convince a judge that they should win the debate. To make this decision, the judge evaluates the affirmative case upholding the resolution and compares it to the negative arguments opposing the resolution.

The affirmative case, or rationale for upholding the values specified in the resolution, consists of the three general lines of argument in value debate. The affirmative side has the burden of proving the three general lines of argument. This argumentative burden stems from the presumption that the resolution is untrue until the affirmative debater convinces the judge otherwise. The negative debater can win the debate by defeating any one of the three general lines of argument. The remainder of the text considers arguments for affirming and denying the general lines of argument in value debate and the conventions for applying these arguments in debate contexts.

Exercises

1. Identify a topicality, criteria, and justification argument that supports each of the following value resolutions:

   Resolved: that patriotism is more important than freedom of expression.
   Resolved: that trade with foreign countries helps maintain the strength of the U.S. economy.
   Resolved: that euthanasia is never justified.

2. Assume that your resolution is "Resolved: that a U.S. foreign policy significantly directed toward the furtherance of human rights is desirable." Which of the following cases would be topical: a case that defends a removal of most-favored nation status for countries involved in human rights abuses; a case that defends increased intervention as a means of overthrowing foreign dictators; and a case that defends an increase in economic assistance to countries that lack the ability to feed their citizenry. Defend your answers.

3. Assume you are arguing against a case that maintains that restrictions on civilian possession of handguns are justified. What off-case arguments could you offer that would compete with the values embodied in the affirmative case?

2

Analyzing Topicality Through Lines of Argument

Chapter Outline

Identifying Key Terms
   Definitions: Implicit or Explicit
   Importance of Definitions
Sources of Definition
   General Dictionaries
   Specialty Dictionaries
   Legislation and Legislative History
   Academic Books and Articles
Standards for Evaluating Competing Definitions
   Grammatical Context
   Each Word Should Have a Meaning
   Reasonable Limits
   Better Definition
   Debatability Standard
Lines of Argument for Affirming Topicality
Claims
   Defining the Terms
   Meeting the Definitions
   Standards for Comparing Competing
     Definitions
Lines of Argument for Denying Topicality Claims
   Failure to Meet Affirmative Definitions
   Failure to Meet Negative Definitions
Lines of Argument for Comparing Topicality
Claims
Summary and Conclusions

Key Terms

topicality
implicit definitions
topicality standards
hasty generalization
whole-resolution argument

Debaters advocating a value-debate resolution must make the claim that the values they defend are the same ones included in the debate resolution. Affirmative debaters have the responsibility to make this argument, known as **topicality.** A topical affirmative case falls within the definitional boundaries of the resolution and does not exceed the scope of the resolution. Affirmative debaters must define, implicitly or explicitly, the key terms of the debate resolution. If they can defend their definitions as acceptable and demonstrate that their value meets these definitions, they are topical. The negative may elect to argue that the affirmative is not topical by indicating that the affirmative definitions are not acceptable or that the affirmative arguments do not meet the definitions.

When you debate, you will discover that both affirmative and negative debaters need to understand the importance of definitions, the process of defining terms, and the standards for evaluating definitions. We outline these issues in the first section of this chapter, because both the affirmative or the negative can use them. Afterwards, we examine the lines of argument available for supporting that the affirmative is topical and the lines of argument for denying that the affirmative is topical. We conclude by identifying the lines of argument you can use to resolve competing topicality claims.

Identifying Key Terms

There is no standard rule for determining which resolutional terms debaters must define. Nevertheless, you should be able to identify potentially controversial terms in any debate resolution. In making that determination, you should expect always to define certain terms that recur in value resolutions. Many terms are likely to be controversial, including the value being affirmed, the method of affirming the value, the value being compared to the affirmative value, and the verb affirming the value.

By contrast, some terms in a resolution are rarely controversial. Noncontroversial terms, which you usually do not need to define, include articles (such as *a, an,* and *the*), the initial terms of all resolutions (i.e., *Resolved: that*), and other terms that do not represent the core of the value debate. However, do not be misled. Occasionally, even seemingly noncontroversial terms may play an important role in a debate about definitions. In the resolution, "Resolved: that increased restrictions on the civilian possession of handguns in the United States would be justified," the term *civilian* generally might be taken to mean *nonmilitary.* Precisely what, however, does *nonmilitary* mean? Does it include police, the Central Intelligence Agency, and other nonmilitary government personnel who may carry weapons? Would a topic addressing restrictions on civilians encompass restrictions on these particular subgroups? These questions would be open to debate despite the apparently obvious meaning of the term.

Affirmative debaters must defend their interpretation of the resolution. Since any word can potentially affect that interpretation, it is vital that you prepare to defend a definition of any and all resolutional terms. Since all definitions have the potential to disprove that a particular case supports the debate topic, the negative debater should investigate the potential definitions of all words in the debate topic.

Definitions: Implicit or Explicit

Some controversy exists regarding when and how the affirmative debater is to define the terms of the resolution. Traditionally, judges have expected affirmative debaters to define terms explicitly at the beginning of the debate. More recently, some debaters have tended to use **implicit definitions**, defending their interpretations only when the negative attacks them. An affirmative debater may implicitly define terms by stating their criteria and justification without explicitly defining terms. Using our previous example of civilian handgun restrictions, an affirmative might implicitly define civilian to include the police by arguing that police departments should be prohibited from carrying handguns on routine patrol.

In the resolution "Resolved: that government censorship of public artistic expression in the United States is an undesirable infringement on individual rights," an affirmative could argue that government censorship of rap music deprives African-Americans of a valuable means of social protest. It could be inferred from their arguments that they were defining "public artistic expression" to include music and "undesirable" to include equal access to rights. The affirmative debaters would still have to defend their definitions, if challenged, but they might not define the words of the resolution explicitly until the negative has attacked or questioned their interpretation of the resolution.

Importance of Definitions

Regardless of whether the affirmative explicitly or implicitly defines the terms of the resolution, all debaters need to realize the importance of the definitions. Definitions regularly determine whether arguments and debates are won or lost. A large number of legislative, executive, and judicial definitions of terms have been important to the ultimate outcome of a decision. In addition, many contract negotiations are devoted to determining a fair and reasonable interpretation of the terms of agreement.

In one of the most notable Supreme Court decisions in the twentieth century, definitions were critical to the outcome. From 1972 to 1974, the Watergate scandal besieged the presidency of Richard M. Nixon. Several operatives of the Committee to Re-elect the President were caught breaking into the Democratic National Committee headquarters at the Watergate Hotel in Washington, D. C. During the re-election campaign and subsequent months, the Nixon administration engaged in a massive cover-up to keep the F.B.I., Congress, and the Office of the Special Prosecutor from uncovering the link between the burglary at Democratic head-quarters and the Committee to Re-elect the President.

Eventually, Congress discovered that President Nixon had been taping all con-versations that occurred in the Oval Office. This practice afforded the Congress and the Office of the Special Prosecutor the opportunity to examine the allegations of a cover-up. When the Office of the Special Prosecutor attempted to obtain the tapes, the President argued that executive privilege and national security permit-ted the executive branch to withhold the tapes.

The case eventually wound up before the Supreme Court. At that point the Office of the Special Prosecutor argued that national security could not be de-fined in such a way that the executive branch could have the authority to elude justice. National security, the prosecutor argued, cannot include subjects of a purely political nature. The administration's interpretation of national security was so broad that it would include any item, including political accountability, that would cast doubt on the integrity of the president. The Supreme Court, with Justice William Rehnquist abstaining, ruled 8–0 that the President was defining national security too broadly and ordered Nixon to turn the tapes over to the Office of the Special Prosecutor. Shortly after the ruling, Nixon resigned his office in disgrace. Unable to sustain his definition of national security in court, Nixon's powerful administration fell.

In addition to political controversy, matters of public policy are frequently influenced by the definition of terms. The meaning of the term *poverty* is fre-quently contested in the halls of Congress and within administrative agencies. The federal government has defined the term *poverty* by establishing a maxi-mum annual income for a family of four. This definition is important because it determines eligibility for federal assistance programs. An individual unable to meet this definition would not qualify for food stamps, Aid for Families with Dependent Children, programs for Women with Infant Children, and other similar programs designed to help the needy. A maximum-income fig-ure has at least two important implications. On the one hand, lowering the figure means fewer people are eligible for poverty programs, and, thus, the funding requirements of the program will be lower. On the other hand, the lower figure means the government can argue that fewer people are in pov-erty and, hence, fewer people need poverty programs. The definition influ-ences who receives assistance, how much money is spent on assistance, and how many people are considered to be in poverty.

In the world of legal and political advocates, definitions frequently determine the results of important decisions. In academic debate, definitions may also influ-ence the decisions reached by judges. The argument of definition is important for three reasons. First, it is necessary to determine if the proposition is probably true or probably false. Second, it is necessary to divide argumentative ground

---

Sample Topical Affirmative

Data: U.S. paramilitary activities in Central America support right-wing
            dictators.
Warrant: Supporting right-wing dictators undermines the credibility of U.S.
            foreign policy.
Claim: Continued U.S. covert involvement in Central America is undesirable.

Sample Nontopical Affirmative

Data: United States conducted a drug war in Central America from 1985–1991.
Warrant: The previous drug war failed.
Claim: Continued U.S. covert involvement in Central America would be
            undesirable.

---

predictably and fairly. And third, it is necessary to decide if the affirmative case supports the resolution.

Accurate definitions are necessary to determine the probable truth of the resolution. If you define terms in such a way that it becomes unclear what the resolution means, then it is difficult for a judge to know if the resolution is probably true. The very meaning of the proposition has to be clearly understood and defined in order to convince a judge to affirm the resolution, For example, in the statement, "Resolved: that continued U.S. covert involvement in Central America would be undesirable," the meaning of "covert involvement" is very debatable. Would covert involvement include paramilitary activities, information collection, business affiliations, and fighting against drugs? The affirmative would need to define what the term means for a judge to decide if covert involvement is undesirable.

Arguments about definitions also are necessary because they confine the issues to arguments that are relevant to the resolution. If, for example, a judge determines that covert involvement does not include the war on drugs, the judge would probably dismiss any arguments that attempted to prove that the war on drugs was undesirable. A judge would only affirm the resolution if the affirmative debater proved that the continued drug war relies on covert involvement. In debate, judges will dismiss arguments not related to the topic; they will listen to all relevant arguments.

The Toulmin model of argumentation illustrates why a critic dismisses arguments that do not support the resolution. In the model above, you can see very clearly how relevant arguments support the claim. Continued paramilitary operations that undermine democracy support the claim that continued U.S. covert involvement would be undesirable. The second example proves that the data and warrant are irrelevant to the claim because the past drug war is not included in "continued U.S. covert involvement." Rather, the affirmative arguments in the second example would not be topical.

Definitions are important in academic debate because debaters can define terms, thereby directing the area of discussion toward arguments favorable to themselves. Since academic debate is also a competitive activity, debaters sometimes attempt to define terms to maximize their strategic options in a given debate round. It has been said that the person who controls the terms of the debate controls the debate. This explains why many debate rounds focus on the definition of terms rather than on issues related to the subject matter of the debate.

Affirmative debaters may sometimes define terms very broadly in order to debate an issue on the periphery of the debate topic. For example, on a recent debate topic, "Resolved: that the American judicial system has overemphasized freedom of the press," negative debaters had many arguments about the value of the free press in a democracy: a free press assures a check on the power of government; a free press provides the public with an avenue for dissenting opinion; and a free press ensures that minority voices are heard. Affirmative debaters attempted to avoid these arguments by defining "freedom of the press" broadly. Broad definitions allowed the affirmative debaters to coopt the advantages generally associated with a free press. They maintained that freedom of the press has led to media monopolies that stifle dissent and minority opinion; freedom of the U.S. press has led to a form of media imperialism in which the views of the United States dominate world opinion; and that freedom of the press has led the public into a false belief that dissent and minority opinion are being heard. In these instances, defining the resolution broadly allowed the affirmative to control the argumentative ground by defining terms to exclude predictable areas of negative arguments.

Sometimes the negative attempts to severely restrict the interpretation of the resolution. They do so in order to narrow the range of possible affirmative defenses of the resolution. Discussing the resolution, "Resolved: that membership in the United Nations is no longer beneficial to the United States," many affirmative debaters elected to identify membership in particular United Nations projects, such as particular United Nations peacekeeping forces or United Nations environmental projects, as no longer beneficial. Some negative teams were able to successfully win the argument that such cases did not meet the requirements of the debate topic. According to these negative debaters, the topic meant that "membership in the United Nations" included all forms of membership, not just a specific type of activity in which the United States took part. This narrow method of defining the resolution restricted the range of possible arguments requiring negative preparation.

Sources of Definition

Many sources exist for defining terms: dictionaries, articles and academic papers, legislative codes and legislative histories, and legal interpretations of terms. When you begin researching a topic, you should examine all sources of definitions in order to determine the various ways they define terms.

Even the number of dictionaries can be surprising. General language dictionaries define terms according to their everyday usage. Some dictionaries include formal definitions for proper usage of terms. Other dictionaries use historical analysis of the language to define terms. Still other dictionaries are specific to a field of study such as politics or law.

General Dictionaries

Many people assume that all general dictionaries are the same. However, that is not the case. For example, Merriam-Webster dictionaries use citations found in printed sources to derive their definitions. Random House dictionaries define terms based on how people use words in daily conversation as well as in some printed matter. The Oxford English Dictionary provides detailed historical accounting of terms with a heavy emphasis on examples of historical origins and usage. Each of these dictionaries will offer the debater differing interpretations of some terms because they rely on differing sources of definition. Consequently, debaters should examine all dictionaries carefully for possible advantageous interpretations of the resolution.

Specialty Dictionaries

When debaters learn what topic they will be debating, they should attempt to discover any dictionaries that might be specific to that field of study. Many academic disciplines have dictionaries specific to their field of study. Additionally, some field-specific dictionaries cross academic disciplines; you should consult these when you know your debate topic. Specialty dictionaries that are very useful for policy debaters include the following:

Black's Law Dictionary

Black's Law Dictionary (*BLD*) is a dictionary of technical legal terms derived from legal opinion and court decisions. Although designed to assist attorneys, debaters should consult *Black's*, given its tendency to include common terms. *Black's* also serves as a bibliographic reference for court cases and legislation relevant to the definitions of terms.

Words and Phrases

Words and Phrases (*W&P*) is a compilation of words and phrases that the United States court system interprets and applies. While technical legal terms are included in these volumes, *Words and Phrases* also includes a large number of non-technical terms found in legislation, contracts, and legal opinion. While *Words and Phrases* identifies and interprets terms, it also cites legal precedent and opinion to justify its interpretations. Debaters should use the citations in *Words and Phrases* to research the court opinion. They can use the reasoning of the courts to justify their interpretation of terms in the debate round.

Corpus Juris Secundum

Corpus Juris Secundum (*CJS*) is a compilation of legal opinion designed to provide attorneys with a reference to determine what court opinions exist in particular subject areas. Much like *Words and Phrases, CJS* includes definitions used by the courts. *CJS* also updates legal interpretations with supplements included in the back of each volume. Debaters should examine *Black's Law Dictionary, Words and Phrases, CJS,* and other legal references because the cases and definitions cited in each source may be different. Each resource offers a variety of definitions that debaters should explore.

Dictionary of Political Science

The *Dictionary of Political Science* is one of many dictionaries specific to the field of political science. Since many debate topics center on important political conflicts, political science dictionaries are frequently a useful resource for debaters. The *Dictionary of Political Science* derives its definitions from articles, textbooks, studies, and published papers in the field of political science.

As this brief listing of specialty dictionaries suggests, there are many sources of definition available in almost every field of study. These dictionaries are frequently among the richest resources available to the debater, as they provide a contextual framework for understanding a field's interpretation of a term. You should attempt to familiarize yourself with any dictionaries that could provide definitions of controversial terms contained in debate topics.

Legislation and Legislative History

Legislators regularly find it necessary to define the terms of their legislation. These definitions are located in congressional hearings, floor debates, and public laws, such as the *Code of Federal Regulations*. To find these resources, locate government depository libraries in your area. In these libraries, you can find reports of congressional hearings on the activity of congressional committees and subcommittees, the *Congressional Record*, which contains debates on the floor of Congress, and all federal laws and regulations. All U.S. citizens are permitted access to such documents.

Academic Books and Articles

Academic authors frequently attempt to narrow their research questions by defining their area of study. Such definitions will serve as fruitful sources of definition for debate. When you research books and articles specific to the topic area, you should remain alert for definitions of resolutional terms that appear in the material. Academic articles, research books, and textbooks all offer definitions of terms usable in debate rounds.

In sum, debaters have a large number of sources to research for definitions of resolutional terms. They have access to many interpretations of debate resolutions. Some of these definitions will undoubtedly be contradictory. When two sides present contradictory definitions in a single debate round, debaters need to be able to defend the appropriateness of their definitions.

Standards for Evaluating Competing Definitions

When attempting to resolve conflicts between competing definitions, debaters can offer standards for evaluating the most appropriate definition for the debate. **Topicality standards** are the criteria used to resolve the conflicts between competing definitions. Standards provide a method for governing how the judge should interpret words in the context of a debate. Without standards for evaluating definitions and topicality arguments, the judge cannot determine which definition should govern the interpretation of the resolution. Many standards are available. We discuss a few prominent ones that recur in competitive collegiate and secondary school debate.

Grammatical Context

One of the most commonly used standards is that the grammatical context of a word should govern the word's meaning. Because many words have such variable interpretations, it is only through their relationship to other words that we can understand their meaning. The resolution, "Resolved: that education has failed at its mission in the United States," illustrates how a word could completely distort the meaning of a resolution if you fail to consider the grammatical context of the sentence. Debaters could define "mission" as a purpose. But "mission" is a broader concept, which applies to a variety of circumstances including religious commitment, places for providing religious instruction, and schoolhouses. A creative affirmative team could argue that public education has forsaken religion, that the educational system does not promote parochial education, and that schoolhouses are built in such a way that they fail educationally. "Mission" is a very general term, which is only understood in relationship to other referents. Without a grammatical standard, debaters could define terms so broadly that the topic would be meaningless and would not offer predictable grounds for debate. It is far better for you to define words in their context than to distort their meaning into another context.

However, debaters occasionally argue that judges should not interpret resolutions according to grammatical standards. First, debaters can argue that strict adherence to grammatical standards restricts the development of language. Language depends on the creativity and invention of authors. Past conventions should not arbitrarily restrict creative thought and invention. Second, debaters can argue that grammar itself evolves. Thus, a strict interpretation of terms and phrases might be an archaic interpretation. Third, debaters can argue that the strict grammatical standard has its origins in an oppressive language system. Many sociologists argue that the upper classes have used strict rules of grammar to reinforce their control and access to societal institutions. Many, for example, argue that standardized admission testing for college represents this approach today because it requires access to the strict rules of grammar to perform well on the Scholastic Aptitude Test and the Graduate Record Examination. Reinforcing the power of the grammatical standard might reinforce the oppression some believe such rules impose. Fourth, the debater can argue that strict adherence to grammar does not improve communication. Some argue that people can communicate without grammar. As long as everyone understands what the debate means, they argue, grammar should not be a valid criterion for evaluating topicality.

Arguments opposed to the grammatical standard are highly problematic. While there is evidence to support each reason that undermines grammar, it may be difficult to convince a judge that strict adherence to grammar decreases creativity, hinders the evolution of language, remains an oppressive tool of the elite, or is unnecessary for effective communication. Academia and other social institutions remain committed to the importance of grammar. Many judges have trouble accepting arguments that grammar is unimportant to communication and understanding. As a result, you should be certain that your interpretation of the debate topic is consistent with grammatical standards of definition.

Each Word Should Have a Meaning

Each word in a sentence should contribute meaning to the interpretation of the sentence. This standard requires debaters to define each word so that it contributes to the interpretation of the resolution. Sometimes it is possible to define a term of the resolution so that other words in the resolution may be devoid of meaning and not serve an important function in the debate. In the resolution, "Resolved: that a unilateral freeze by the United States on nuclear weapons production and development would be desirable," an affirmative debater could argue that adherence to the Nuclear Nonproliferation Treaty or holding arms control talks with China would be desirable. However, such an interpretation ignores that the Nuclear Nonproliferation Treaty and arms control talks are multilateral actions, not unilateral, or one-sided, actions. By defending such an example, the affirmative makes the word "unilateral" a meaningless term in the resolution. A judge would probably conclude that the affirmative case is not topical because it ignores the meaning of "unilateral" in the resolution. If debaters define terms in such a way that words become meaningless, they alter the fundamental grounds of the debate. Judges usually reject such definitions.

There are reasons why each word in a resolution should not have its own independent meaning. In some resolutions there may be words that provide no unique meaning. For example, in the resolution, "Resolved: that any and all injury resulting from the disposal of hazardous waste should be the legal responsibility of the producer of the waste," some might maintain that the phrase "any and all" has one meaning. Each word only reinforces the meaning of the other because if a producer is responsible for *any* injury the producer would, therefore, be responsible for *all* injuries.

The point here is not that "any" and "all" are synonymous, but that their combined effect is to underline a single standard. If a professor tells you, "You are responsible for all material because any and all subjects could be included on the test," the words "any and all" only reinforce the teacher's message that you are responsible for one hundred percent of the material. The combination of terms allows for emphasis, but robs "any" of its ability to designate particular areas of study. As a student you need to be ready to answer any question on any subject since all of them can be tested.

Reasonable Limits

Another standard debaters frequently employ to determine the appropriate definition is whether the definition sets a reasonable limit on argumentative ground. If debaters define the resolution too broadly, the negative will not be able to predict possible affirmative cases. Such an interpretation would be unreasonable. In defense of the resolution, "Resolved: that violence is a justified response to political oppression," an affirmative team could argue that violence is justified in the cases of Palestinians in the occupied territories, black South Africans, Chinese students, and other oppressed groups around the world. The affirmative would probably be able to argue that any one of these groups is an example of a people suffering political oppression. Some believe that the nation of Israel lives under the political oppression of the Arab nations, that Northern Irish Catholics live under the political oppression of the British government, or that all peoples of the world live under the political oppression of the nations with nuclear weapons. Within the framework of these definitions, debaters could argue that any group that lives under the threat of war suffers political oppression. Others might argue that prisoners in overcrowded conditions are politically oppressed, that Americans living under capitalism are oppressed by a politically sanctioned economic system, that refugees being held as detainees are politically oppressed, and many other groups could be considered politically oppressed. These interpretations, while supportable with evidence, make the resolution very broad and unpredictable. Negatives could mount a persuasive case that these definitions are unreasonable.

If a narrow interpretation of a term resulted in only a very few possible cases, it might also be unreasonable. In defense of the resolution about political oppression, affirmative debaters could argue that political oppression can only refer to internal oppression by governments against members of their own populations. By narrowing the ground for the debate to such a small handful of cases, a negative debater could easily argue that the term is being defined too narrowly to be reasonable.

Better Definition

It is very difficult for a debate judge to determine what constitutes a reasonable interpretation of a debate resolution. Some debate judges and debaters argue that a better-definition standard is preferable to the reasonableness standard. Those advocating the better-definition standard argue that to impose the vague reasonableness standard does not create a meaningful way to choose a definition. Instead, they argue that the better definition defended in the debate should be the winning definition.

There is no consistently applied standard for what constitutes a better definition. Debaters can argue that the more limiting definition is better because it ensures in-depth discussion. Debaters could argue that the broader definition is better because debaters learn about more subjects through an expanded topic. Debaters could argue that the better definition is the one that has the most authoritative support. Debaters can conceive of many arguments about why one definition is better than another.

Debatability Standard

Many debaters and judges find the better-definition standard problematic. Some argue that there is no difference between the better definition and the reasonable definition. A more reasonable interpretation, after all, would be better in most debates. Others argue that if the better-definition standard is taken to its extreme, it will overly restrict the subject matter of the debate. In place of the vague reasonableness standard and the restrictive better-definition standard, some argue that a standard that results in fair and focused debates is the only meaningful measure of acceptability for a definition.

Debaters can level the same criticisms against the debatability standard as those used against all other standards. The meaning of the standard is open to discussion and may be difficult to determine objectively. What is a fair and focused debate? How can a judge use such a standard to evaluate the appropriateness of definitions for the resolution?

Having established potential sources of definitions and standards to assess those definitions, the remainder of this chapter will identify the lines of argument used to affirm or deny the topicality of a case and to resolve conflicts between the two. In the process of developing these lines of argument, both affirmative and negative debaters should borrow from the sources and standards we have just discussed. Depending on the argumentative circumstances of each debate, either team could discover that a given standard or source of definition would benefit the persuasive force of their positions.

Lines of Argument for Affirming Topicality Claims

In order to defend their proposal as a topical interpretation of the resolution, affirmative debaters must be prepared to make three arguments. First, they must define terms; second, they must prove that their defense of the resolution falls within the definitions they provide; and third, they must support their interpretations of terms according to defensible standards.

ESTABLISHING DEFINITIONS

In the final round of the 1990 Cross-Examination Debate Association National Championships, Central State University of Oklahoma (Charles Mallard and Josh Hoe) affirmed the resolution "Resolved: that the trend toward increasing foreign investment in the United States is detrimental to this nation." Southwest Missouri State University (Robert Olson and Eric Morris) negated the resolution. Central State argued that foreign investment encourages economic growth, which ultimately harms the environment. To defend their interpretation of the resolution, Mr. Mallard presented the following definitions.

First Affirmative

One, foreign, Random House Dictionary defines in 1987. "Foreign: of, pertaining to, or derived from another country or nation; not native" (p. 749).

Two, investment. Corpus Juris Secundum defines in 1981.

The word "investment" generally is used to describe the employment of capital for the purpose of obtaining income or profit. In its most comprehensive sense, it is understood to signify the laying out of money in such a manner that it may produce revenue whether the particular method be a loan or the purchase of stocks, notes, securities or other property (p. 215).

Three, detrimental. Corpus Juris Secundum defines in 1956. "The word detrimental means not for the best interest of" (p. 925).

Four, nation. Ballantine's Law Dictionary defines in 1969. A nation. "A body politic or society of mankind united together for the purpose of promoting their mutual safety and advantage by their combined strength, occupying a definite territory and politically organized under one government" (p. 830). All other terms we feel are self-evident and are operationally defined through the application of case.

Defining the Terms

Earlier in the chapter, we identify many sources of definitions. Relying on these sources, debaters should research definitions that are consistent with their defense of the resolution. As we discussed at the beginning of the chapter, debaters can implicitly define the terms. However, if their implicit definitions are challenged, they need to be prepared with defensible definitions. You can define the terms of your resolution in two ways: by explaining what the definition includes and by specifying what the definition excludes.

When you identify what a term includes, you begin the process of setting definitional boundaries. You show what qualities or attributes are present. In the resolution, "Resolved: that government censorship of public artistic expression in the United States is an undesirable infringement on individual rights," the term "public" suggests to many experts in the field that the artistic expression must be funded by a government source. If the affirmative defines "public" in such a fashion, the topic would include any grant by the National Endowment for the Arts or similar state grants.

While explaining what is included in a definition is useful, sometimes indicating what is excluded from the definition is necessary for a full understanding of the concept. By eliminating similar concepts that might easily be confused with a term, definition by exclusion adds precision to a term's meaning. Our previous definition of public excludes all artistic expression that is not funded by the government. It would eliminate, for example, any consideration of government efforts to censor pornographic movies from the airwaves because the government did not fund those projects. By excluding all forms of artistic expression not funded by government sources, the affirmative's definition has effectively limited the meaning of the sentence as a whole.

Meeting the Definitions

Because many definitions of resolutional terms exist, affirmative debaters must decide which definitions are most consistent with the affirmative case. Affirmative debaters should be able to prove that their defense of the resolution is consistent with the definitions they are willing and able to defend. Affirmatives should avoid offering arguments to affirm the resolution that does not fulfill their own definition of terms. For example, in the resolution, "Resolved: that the United States is justified in providing military support to nondemocratic governments," an affirmative debater might define "nondemocratic" to mean any nation that does not have fair and free elections. If the same affirmative team then tried to prove the resolution true with an example of military support to a country such as Australia or Canada that does hold fair and free elections, they would not meet their own definition.

However absurd it may seem, poorly prepared affirmative debaters can make a mistake by failing to meet their own definition of terms. Affirmative debaters can prevent this mistake by being thorough in their preparation and certain that they can meet their own definition. Some ways to increase the likelihood that the affirmative case fulfills the affirmative definition include using definitions from the primary articles in the affirmative case area, finding examples of the definition that are similar to or include the affirmative case area, and finding evidence that discusses the affirmative proposal in relationship to the language of the debate topic.

Standards for Comparing Competing Definitions

Regardless of what definition affirmatives use, they need to defend the appropriateness of their definitions. In order to accomplish this objective, affirmatives can defend a standard for evaluating the definitions and prove that their definitions meet the standard. Affirmative debaters are well advised to construct their cases around the core issues of the debate topic in order to maximize the argument that their interpretations are appropriate.

Always remember that topicality arguments are offered to a judge who has his or her own opinions on the meaning of the resolution. While you can expect any trained debate judge to evaluate a debate based on arguments offered in that contest, judges are more likely to find "reasonable" those definitions that come closest to traditional interpretations. Standards that run counter to important touchstones such as grammar and context should be used with caution, and only then when carefully explained.

Affirmatives improve their chances of persuading the judge that their interpretation of the debate topic is correct if they are able to meet restrictive standards. Meeting restrictive standards allows affirmatives to argue that their definitions are rigorous, qualifying their case even under very strict interpretive rules. Affirmatives do not automatically lose when they cannot meet the strictest standards, but they do forfeit an important persuasive resource. Suppose, for example, that the affirmative debaters were unable to meet the common standards of grammatical context and independent meaning. Lacking these standards, they could only argue that grammar is unimportant or that each word does not have to have independent meaning. Because most judges think that grammatical context and the independent meaning of words *are* important standards, affirmative definitions that meet these two standards are likely to be more persuasive than arguments about whether the standards are inappropriate for the debate. Affirmative debaters might argue that their interpretation of the resolution meets any number of the limiting standards listed previously: that they offer a reasonable interpretation of the resolution; that their interpretation allows for a debatable topic; and that their definition is better because it provides the better limit in the debate.

If the affirmative interpretation of the resolution is grammatically correct, provides meaning for all words in the debate topic, and narrows the ground of argument more appropriately than the definition offered by the negative debaters, it is very likely the better definition. Affirmative debaters should always remember that if the definition they elect to defend meets the standards demanded by the negative, they have no reason to establish standards of their own for the topicality argument. The affirmative debaters can efficiently answer their opponent's argument by accepting the standards and definitions offered by the negative and proceeding to meet those standards.

Lines of Argument for Denying Topicality Claims

Because many affirmative debaters elect to define terms implicitly rather than explicitly, it is often necessary for the negative debater to initiate the argument that the affirmative case does not fall within the definitional boundaries of the resolution. To argue that the affirmative is not topical, the negative debaters have two options. Initially, they can show how the affirmative arguments fail to meet the definition of terms of the resolution as defined by the affirmative. They can also argue that the affirmative fails to meet alternative definitions that yield a superior interpretation of the resolution.

Failure to Meet Affirmative Definitions

Usually the simplest means for showing that the affirmative is not topical is proving that the affirmative's interpretation of the resolution does not fall within its own definitions. Here, the negative concedes that the affirmative team has properly defined the terms of the resolution. No standards for definitions are needed, as both teams agree that the affirmative definitions are appropriate. The argument occurs when the negative shows that the specifics of the affirmative's interpretation do not fall within the limits established by the affirmative.

Assume that the resolution stated, "Resolved: that continued U.S. covert involvement in Central America would be undesirable." An affirmative team advocating this resolution might define "covert involvement" to mean actions conducted in secret. The same team might justify the resolution by discussing the failures of the policy to aid the contras in their attempted overthrow of the Sandinista regime in Nicaragua. They might argue that the Reagan administration's policy of aiding the contra rebels caused massive human suffering in Nicaragua.

In this situation, negative debaters might well concede that "covert involvement" means actions conducted in secret. However, given that continual news coverage, congressional hearings, and members of the executive branch all discussed the contra-aid effort in great detail, the effort could hardly be called secret. Because the effort was not conducted in secret, it violates the affirmative's own definition of the topic.

Failure to Meet Negative Definitions

Since many affirmative debaters elect to define terms implicitly rather than explicitly, it is frequently necessary for the negative debater to initiate the argument that the affirmative's interpretations of the resolution exceed the definitional boundaries of the resolution. Even if the negative debaters do not have to initiate the topicality argument, they may think that the affirmative definitions do not define the topic properly. In either case, negative debaters should familiarize themselves with four lines of argument to show that the affirmative is not topical: 1) they can offer their own definitions of the key terms of the resolution; 2) they can establish standards for evaluating the competing definitions that show the superiority of negative definitions; 3) they can prove that the affirmative's interpretations do not fall within the negative's definition of the topic; or 4) they can show that the affirmative's interpretation is not representative of the resolution as a whole.

TOPICALITY ARGUMENT

Robert Olson of Southwest Missouri State University offered the following alternative interpretation of the resolution against Central State. Josh Hoe answered the argument in the accompanying speech.

First Negative

[T]he first off-case position will be topicality. The A Subpoint is standards. Little one [interpretations] must be grammatically consistent (Parsons and Barbs say in 87). The definition of the affirmative must be consistent with their grammatical use in the prepositional sentence. Whether a word is used as a noun or a verb will substantially alter the meaning of the preposition.

Two subpoint is that this is the same as written language (Porter Parren in 1959). But written English is not a different language from spoken English.

Last subpoint is, must be grammatical to be reasonable, meaning reasonableness [standards] do not [overwhelm grammar] (Professor Katsulas in 1985). "Another way that the negative could prove the affirmative's definitions are unreasonable is to demonstrate that there is an absence of grammatical context."

Four is, must be within limits of criteria, i.e., if you cannot [identify detriments to this nation] within affirmative, then you will cross-apply it to topicality.

B Subpoint is violations. First, is that "is" only indicates present tense. Words and Phrases in 1964: "The word 'is' constitutes the third person singular of the present indicative of the verb "to be." It is employed only in indication of the present tense."

Second Affirmative

First of all, he says that grammar must be consistent. [T]hat is his interpretation of grammar. . . . [We are] indicating that there are other possible grammatical interpretations. . . . [W]hen there are two possible interpretations of the grammar then we don't violate grammar rules, right? Which is what he is trying to argue. He says it must be the same as written language. That's fine with me. He says it must be grammatical to be consistent. But we . . . [argue that our interpretation is] grammatical through a different interpretation.

He says must be within the criteria. . . . We . . . indicate that this is not true . . . [The negative argument] collaps[es] burdens. He's indicating that we have to show you [a] probablis[tic justification] to indicate that we are topical, which is a misnomer. And it's not true.

Independently, I would indicate that you should not presume intent. . . . The negative is not the appointed guardian of the resolution, and there's no reason to presume their interpretation correct.

The next argument is that just because we are limited does not necessarily make us nontopical. That is all I need there.

I am off the violation. His first argument is that "is" equals the present tense. Obviously, he was not listening to case. [The evidence from] Holdgate in 89 tells you that there are wars occurring now over resources which would indicate that we meet this violation. [The value is being compromised in the present tense.]

(Continued)

TOPICALITY ARGUMENT—Continued

First Negative (Cont.)

Last is two, . . . affirmative usage is false to fact, i.e., if you assume it is anything besides present tense, you're describing it as being constantly this way, as static; that's false to fact link. Lee explains in 1941: "When a form of the verb to be connects a noun to an adjective, we invariably express a false-to-fact relationship. In its simplest and sharpest form this can be seen in the sentence: The leaf is green, the picture is ugly, the speech was trite, and its kind, et cetera."

The B Subpoint, the last subpoint is little three and that is implications. The detriment must be consistent with [the] proper [purpose] of the investment]. [You can] cross-apply criteria, because they argue life is absolute. Not my life or your life, but everyone's life, and certainly we aren't all dead, right? [Thus, according to their criteria and our definition, they do not meet the conditions of present tense required of the word "is."]

C Subpoint is impacts, that is voting issue. First of all, it is traditionally a voting issue, I would also suggest that it is jurisdictional, and Patterson and Zarefsky think it is a voting issue, too.

Second Affirmative (Cont.)

Independently, we are reading evidence that says pretty clearly that heat deaths are occurring now. When he doesn't get to this on case [he drops an important argument proving we are topical].

Off of his second argument, that it's false to fact. [F]irst argument is that "is" is determined by context. Corpus Juris Secundum argues in 54: "However it has also been said that, by reason of context, the meaning of the word may not be confined to the present."

The next argument is that the word "toward" implies the movement toward, and this is . . . from the same source. "In the sense toward or towards is defined as meaning in the course of line leading to [or] with direction to."

The next argument is that increasing means getting larger. Random House argues in 87. "Growing larger or greater, emerging, augmenting"

The next argument is that the trend implies movement towards. 2001 Business Terms argues in 1987: "The general movement of something, such as commodity prices or power consumption, in a particular direction over a period of time."

The next and final argument is that "is" becomes "will be" within this context. This is Corpus Juris Secundum again in 54. "But it may have future signification in the sense of 'will be' or 'shall be.' " Therefore, the movement over a period of time leading to something larger will be detrimental. [Within the grammatical structures of this sentence, future impacts still prove that foreign investment is detrimental in the present.]

Alternative Definitions

The negative can win the topicality argument by successfully maintaining that the affirmative interpretation of the resolution is unacceptable. The negative can argue that the affirmative's interpretation is too broad or too narrow. However, it is far more persuasive for the negative debater to maintain that not only is the affirmative definition unacceptable, but that a more acceptable definition is available. If the affirmative definition is the *only* definition in the debate, a judge may be persuaded to accept that definition even if it is unreasonably broad or narrow. By offering an alternative definition, the negative provides the judge with a rationale for dismissing an unreasonable affirmative interpretation.

Establishing Standards

Having defined the terms of the resolution, the negative debater needs to identify standards for how the judge should evaluate competing definitions. The most common standards (grammatical context, each word has meaning, reasonability, better definition, and debatability) have already been discussed. The negative debater should choose to defend the standard(s) that provide(s) the rationale for rejecting the affirmative's interpretation of the resolution. For example, does the affirmative's interpretation ignore grammatical rules? If so, the negative can encourage the judge to consider grammatical concerns when assessing the affirmative's interpretation.

Choosing the appropriate standard is critical to the negative's ability to convince the judge that an affirmative's case falls outside the scope of the resolution. Consider the resolution, "Resolved: that membership in the United Nations is no longer beneficial to the United States." When debaters used this resolution in the past, many negative teams chose to employ the grammatical standards for assessing topicality. These debaters argued that the word "membership," being singular, means that the only grammatically acceptable interpretation of membership must mean the complete and total membership of the United States. This interpretation excluded membership in individual elements of the United Nations. By emphasizing the grammatical standard in these debates, many negative debaters were able to convince judges that affirmative teams who limited discussion to United States involvement in particular facets of the United Nations did not fulfill the terms of the resolution.

If these same debaters had relied on the reasonable limits standard instead, their chance for success would have diminished. Would it be unreasonable for affirmatives to expect negative debaters to prepare individual arguments on each of the finite number of U.N. activities in which the United States is engaged? Probably not. Even if the affirmative could make a case that United States membership in particular facets of the United Nations is no longer desirable, the negative could easily anticipate the range of possible interpretations. Peacekeeping forces, UNICEF, and the U.N. Security Council are examples of facets of the U.N. that are predictable. A debater who relied upon the reasonable limits standard, then, would have a difficult time convincing a judge that the affirmative's effort to limit discussion to some aspect of U.N. membership was not topical.

The point here is that negative speakers need to choose their strategies carefully. Not all standards apply equally well in all cases. You need to look at your options and decide which approach or approaches will be most productive in a given set of circumstances.

In addition to making the right choice of argument, debaters must also explain the argument fully. If, for example, the negative believes the affirmative is violating the standard that each word should have meaning, then the negative should argue why such a standard is necessary for debate. The negative debater should illustrate how the affirmative renders a term of the resolution meaningless, offer an alternative definition that gives each word meaning, and explain how the definition meets the standard.

If the negative believes the affirmative unfairly broadens the debate topic, it should pick one of the three limitation standards for debate (reasonability, better definition, debatability). Having selected a standard, the negative should explain how the affirmative violates the standard, offer an alternative definition that meets the standard, and explain how the negative definition meets the standard. Through this process, the negative explains to the judge the proper interpretation of the resolution *and* the standards that explain the interpretation.

Establishing Nontopicality of the Affirmative Proposal

By offering alternative definitions and defending standards that provide a rationale for accepting those definitions, the negative offers its own persuasive interpretation of the resolution. The remaining step for proving nontopicality is to explain why the affirmative's case falls outside of this interpretation. In the resolution, "Resolved: that the trend toward increasing foreign investment in the United States is detrimental to this nation," the negative must determine if the affirmative case actually deals with a "trend toward increasing foreign investment." Relying on a reasonableness standard and a mainstream definition of "trend," the negative could easily conclude that increasing investment by a large investor like Japan reflects a trend and is therefore topical. On the other hand, a few more investments by a nation with a weak economy and minimal holdings of U.S. property, such as Mexico, would probably not constitute a "trend" toward increasing investment. At best, Mexico could engage in sporadic financial dealings that would fall short of an actual trend.

On a few occasions, the negative can avoid the trouble of establishing its own interpretation of the resolution. A few affirmative debaters will offer a set of definitions that do not encompass their specific case. In these instances, the only responsibility of the negative is to explain why the affirmative plan falls outside of the affirmative's own interpretation. No alternative definitions or standards are necessary.

Arguing Hasty Generalization or Whole Resolution

At times, the affirmative may define a term so narrowly that the judge cannot infer the probable truth of the resolution. The negative argues, in effect, that the example the affirmative is using to justify the resolution is not sufficiently representative to affirm the resolution. Assume for a moment that your school cafeteria serves a good grilled cheese sandwich. It would be hasty to conclude from the one sandwich that your cafeteria is a good restaurant. **Hasty generalization** is an argument that suggests that the affirmative justification is not sufficiently representative for anyone to infer the probable truth of the debate topic. (See the discussion of the hasty generalization fallacy in Chapter Six of the core volume.)

A similar argument to hasty generalization is the whole-resolution argument. The **whole resolution argument** suggests that the purpose of nonpolicy debate is to examine the probable truth or probable falsity of the general claim of the value resolution. The argument asserts that the affirmative has the responsibility to defend the entirety of the resolution. In the example of the school cafeteria, someone could defeat your claim that the cafeteria is a good restaurant by showing that the salad bar is weak. In order to sustain your argument, you would have to show that the sandwiches, entrees, and salad bar are all good, making the cafeteria a good restaurant.

Hasty generalization and whole-resolution arguments place the burden of proof on the negative to initiate the arguments. First, the negative must define terms as in any topicality argument. Second, the negative must prove that the affirmative is a minor subset of the topic compared to more substantial concerns. Usually, the negative has to establish some standard for determining whether or not the affirmative example can be generalized sufficiently to affirm the resolutional statement. Third, the negative must convince judges that the resolution should be negated rather than affirmed because of a minor example. The negative debaters must persuade the judge that the resolution can and should be judged as a general statement rather than a specific statement.

In the resolution, "Resolved: that the United States Supreme Court, on balance, has granted excessive power to law enforcement agencies," an affirmative debater might argue that the Court granted too much power to the police when it allowed the police to search containers found in automobiles during routine traffic stops. An affirmative debater might argue that this practice unreasonably expands the police power of the state and further erodes the privacy rights of U.S. citizens. A negative debater, rather than argue the truth or falsity of the argument, may elect to argue that one cannot infer from one search and seizure decision that the Supreme Court has, on balance, granted excessive power to law enforcement.

The negative debater who wishes to argue hasty generalization or whole resolution in this instance would first have to define the important terms to determine what "excessive power to law enforcement agencies" includes. A definition that includes search and seizure would be a good definition since it encompasses the affirmative example but does not exclude other decisions the Court has made. Second, the negative debater would want to point out that many search and seizure decisions have been made and that such decisions do not grant "excessive" power to law enforcement. Negative debaters would want to find evidence supporting their position that the broad range of search and seizure decisions have resulted in nonexcessive power. Having established that the affirmative is generalizing too broadly from a single example, the negative debater would finally have to convince a judge that the hasty generalization or whole-resolution argument warrants a rejection of the resolution.

Lines of Argument for Comparing Topicality Claims

As in all other debate arguments, debaters who compare competing topicality arguments and resolve the conflict between the arguments will more successfully persuade the judge as to the merits of their position. The lines of argument approach suggests several questions that debaters can use to help resolve competing topicality claims.

Can the resolution be defined to include the affirmative case? The affirmative debaters must be able to prove that their interpretation of terms actually meets the requirements of the resolution. The negative debaters, usually by offering alternative definitions, attempt to argue that the affirmative is not fulfilling the requirements of the resolution. If the negative debaters can convince the judge that the affirmative case does not fall within the scope of the debate topic, they will probably win the debate.

Can the affirmative interpretation of the resolution fall within the definition of the resolution offered by the negative? At times, the affirmative debaters may be able to argue that their defense of the resolution is consistent with the negative definition of the resolution. If the affirmative debaters can prove that their interpretation of the resolution can fulfill the requirements of the negative interpretation as well as their own, then the affirmative team will probably win the topicality argument.

What are the optimal standards for evaluating competing definitions of resolutional terms? No single rule applies in all cases. Both sides will probably offer persuasive topicality standards for the debate. For example, on the topic, "Resolved: that membership in the United Nations is no longer beneficial to the United States," we saw how negative debaters were often successful in holding affirmatives to a "whole membership" standard, effectively eliminating cases that dealt instead with some facet of the nation's membership in the U.N. The argument was not, of course, universally successful. Some speakers were able to persuade a judge that a grammatical interpretation of the resolution did not require the affirmative to defend the entire gamut of U.N. membership. Nevertheless, many of these debaters could not persuade the judge that grammar should be the only standard, or even the most important standard. The grammatical standard arguably overlimited the debate topic because only one affirmative justification would be topical: the affirmative must prove that it is no longer beneficial for the United States to be a full member in the United Nations. Many teams were able to argue that such a standard destroys debatability and should be rejected. Conflict between standards means that debaters must persuade the judge that their standards are more appropriate in any specific debate.

Are the definitions consistent with the optimal standards for evaluation? At the end of the debate, the judge must decide if the definitions meet the standards. A debater could conceivably win the argument that his or her standards should govern the debate, but then lose the argument that the chosen definition fulfills the standards. For example, a debater could argue for a grammatical standard and then read a definition of a noun in place of an adverb. Or the debater could argue for a reasonable limit standard and then read a definition that is unreasonable.

Debaters need to understand that a standard is only effective in a particular context. The debater must be able to show that the rule matches with the example provided by the resolution. At the simplest level, topicality arguments are a sophisticated form of sense-making. Your topicality arguments will probably be at their best if you are satisfied that your position genuinely makes sense out of the terms in the resolution.

Does the affirmative case have to fulfill all of the terms of the resolution? In addition to establishing that the affirmative is not topical, the negative should be prepared to argue that fulfilling the terms of the resolution is necessarily a voting issue. Many affirmative debaters have argued that they do not have to fulfill all of the terms of the resolution. In short, affirmative debaters have been known to argue that topicality is not a voting issue. These debaters assume that they meet the goal of the debate topic if the affirmative debates a subject matter germane to the resolution. As long as the negative has adequate opportunity to prepare for such a debate, the goals of the debate topic remain intact. Rigid adherence to the topicality argument is not necessary.

There are several problems with this approach to topicality arguments. First, many debate judges find it wholly unpersuasive and may even take offense at its use. Arguing positions that many judges find unacceptable violates all tenets of audience analysis and persuasion. Second, topicality is traditionally a voting issue, which is perhaps why so many judges take offense at the suggestion that the affirmative does not have to support the resolution. Many national debate tournaments, including the Cross-Examination Debate Association National Tournament, the National Debate Tournament, and tournaments sponsored by the American Debate Association, require topicality to be a voting issue. The norm clearly expressed through the traditional institutions of competitive academic debate indicates that topicality is a voting issue.

Third, there are theoretical considerations that justify the argument that topicality is a voting issue. Affirmative debaters begin the debate advocating the resolution. As a result, any arguments they make should support that resolution. To argue at some point that the resolution is irrelevant makes the initial affirmative argument irrelevant and renders any negative arguments against the resolution irrelevant. Any arguments that are not relevant to the resolution are usually ignored by the debate judge. As the illustrations of the Toulmin model point out, irrelevant data and warrants do not support the resolutional claim.

Fourth, there are many analogies that give support to the claim that topicality is a voting issue. Analogies may be a weak form of argument but, in this instance, they may provide some understanding of the reasons topicality is a voting issue. Jurisdictional analogies are available. Courts, congressional committees, and administrative agencies frequently dismiss cases that are not within their jurisdiction. Some debaters argue that debate judges should also dismiss cases that fall outside of their "jurisdiction." The analogy of the social contract can also justify the argument that topicality is a voting issue. Many debaters borrow from political philosophy and adopt a social contract theory of debate participation. In democratic governments, individuals enter into a de facto social contract to abide by the rules and laws of the society's elected representatives. In exchange, they receive essential services such as the administration of justice, enforcement of public peace and welfare, and the national defense. Similarly, some debaters argue that by agreeing to debate a resolution, debaters have entered into a social contract to abide by the words of the resolution.

Fifth, and finally, real-world implications can justify topicality as a voting issue. As we pointed out at the beginning of this chapter, there are many historical examples where the meaning of words were essential to resolving important disputes. Defining terms too broadly or too narrowly can lead to negative consequences. If policymakers were to use the same definitions and rationales as affirmative debaters, what would be the implications? If a debater can indicate that a definition can have important implications for public policy, topicality arguments become more than a mere semantic game.

Has the affirmative created a hasty generalization or failed to prove that a holistic perspective justifies the resolution? An affirmative debater faced with the hasty generalization argument has at least four reasonable options for answering the argument. First, the debater could defeat the negative definition. In the law enforcement example, the affirmative debaters could argue that the decision they are attacking granted excessive power. Other decisions might have granted power, but only this decision granted excessive power. The negative definition, therefore, is irrelevant since it defines "power," but not "excessive power."

Second, the affirmative could argue that the affirmative is representative of the resolution. If the only question is "has the Court granted excess power," answering that question requires the use of examples. The only way one can determine if the Court has granted too much power to law enforcement is to examine the decisions of the Court and the effects of those decisions. If one example can be proven representative, then it might be sufficient to argue that the affirmative is representative.

Third, the affirmative debater could argue that the resolution as defined by the negative is probably true. That is, the affirmative could agree with the negative requirement that more representative evidence is necessary to demonstrate that the resolution is probably true and proceed to offer that evidence. If more search and seizure decisions have contributed to the granting of excessive power to law enforcement agencies, the affirmative could read evidence indicating that this is true, point out that it is consistent with the initial example, and consequently, meet the negative requirement for more representative examples.

TOPICALITY ARGUMENT

In the final round of the 1988 Cross Examination Debate Association National Championships, Southern Illinois University (John Lapham and Mark West) affirmed the resolution, "Resolved: that the American judicial system has overemphasized freedom of the press." William Jewel College (Raymond Roberts and David Israelite) negated the resolution. Southern Illinois urged adoption of the resolution because the judicial system has held that citizens have no guaranteed right of access insuring that their views are printed in newspapers. Southern Illinois contended that without guaranteed access, the views of ecologists receive little support in the popular media. William Jewell argued that this form of argument ignored the probable truth of the entire resolution. Some access may be denied for a few groups but that does not justify the conclusion that the judicial system has overemphasized freedom of the press generally. Mr. Roberts presents the negative position and Mr. West responds.

First Negative

Off case observation number one will be in terms of whole resolution. I'll tell you in terms of (A) Subpoint standards. One subpoint intent of CEDA is whole resolution. Tomlison explains in 1983: "Another hallmark of CEDA has been to ask debaters to remember the intent of the resolution. These are qualities to be retained by any CEDA round. To ignore them is to reject the basic philosophy of the organization."

Two subpoint under this is the focus of CEDA is on the resolution. CEDA yearbook in 1987 explains. "The debate is limited to determining the truth of the resolution whether it is one value, a fact, or pseudo-policy." In other words we're talking whole-resolution here.

(B) Subpoint, violations. I will tell you first of all that the affirmative is only talking about ecological impacts and only talking about ecological access. On that level not talking about entirety of the resolution. And I think that becomes very clear in

Second Affirmative

I would like to begin with the off case observation on the whole resolution. I would begin with the (A) Subpoint. My first response is that you should have a reasonable interpretation. If we are arguing that the entire autonomous press is bad that is certainly examining the entire resolution.

My second argument is that access is an extremely common case and when examining the topic and when examining general access cases that would be a common interpretation that the whole resolution can and should be allowed.

On the (B) Subpoint where they argue violations. They only say we're only talking about ecological access and therefore we are not whole resolution. My first argument is that this is not true. We are talking about the entire system of preventing access by the autonomous press. So the violation in and of itself is incorrect.

My second argument is that we are also arguing that free press is bad. It is a very simple holistic interpretation of the topic and I don't understand the violation. I don't think it's prima

(Continued)

TOPICALITY ARGUMENT—Continued

First Negative (Cont.)

cross-examination when David stands up here and tells you "OK, we're talking about access, right? Well, yes, no." Again, only a very narrow part of the resolution. On that level, I would say,

(C) Subpoint that this violates. It's a prima facia issue and should be a voting issue this round.

Second Affirmative (Cont.)

facially a violation because they only say we're talking about ecological access which is not correct.

My third argument is that the Schmidt evidence we give you under observation one says that always the Supreme Court has held there is no right to access. If that is not a whole resolutional analysis throughout history I don't know what is.

My fourth argument is that additionally the Smith evidence that we provide under observation one says that they even go beyond not allowing access and that they prevent the legislature from allowing access. That is certainly an overactive American judicial system and a broad interpretation.

The fifth argument is that the Barron evidence, that is not discussed either under observation one, says that there is a general trend to the future and how access will be denied.

The final argument is that if they demand a Supreme Court case that is specific to the environment I will provide one to determine that specifically that the environment is provided for as well. Goldstein argues in 1986 the environment and how the Supreme Court has prevented environmental access. " The court's present posture on Freedom of Speech and advertising was defined most clearly in 1980 in Central Hudson . . . The court held the government interest in conserving energy, while important, could not overcome the utility's right to free speech."

Finally, the affirmative could argue that hasty generalization and whole-resolution arguments are not valid for rejecting the probable truth of the affirmative's defense of the resolution. The affirmative could argue that examples are acceptable. Our affirmative could argue that one example is sufficient to prove that the Court granted "excessive power." They could argue that if a resolution is true in a given instance, then the negative cannot disprove the resolution by proving that there are some instances in which it is not true. Because the court did not grant excessive power in all cases does not mean that the Court did not grant excessive power. The affirmative could also argue that the negative is creating an impossible burden for the affirmative. The affirmative could argue that it is impossible to come to a general decision about whether or not a debatable resolution is probably true or probably false. The only purpose of debate is to decipher the circumstances in which the resolution is true and identify the circumstances in which it is false. If the affirmative identifies the instances in which it is true, then they have fulfilled their burden.

Summary and Conclusions

Topicality is a fundamental argument in academic debate. In order to uphold the resolution, a judge must be clear as to its meaning. In order to provide fair argumentative ground in a competitive debate, it is important to have some degree of predictability to the debate topic. Debaters should strive to understand and apply the topicality argument and its defenses when and where appropriate. Several important lines of argument aid the development, coherence, and clarity of topicality arguments.

First, debaters must understand the processes of definition. When debaters learn what topic they will be debating, it is very important that they familiarize themselves with the definitions generally available in dictionaries, legal and legislative documents, and academic articles and books. The affirmative needs to know what definitions exist to determine if their interpretation falls within acceptable perspectives of what the resolution means. Definitions can identify both what is included and what is excluded in discussions of the topic. Negative debaters need to know ways an affirmative might defend the resolution to determine where they should focus the bulk of their preparation.

Second, debaters need to familiarize themselves with the standards available for evaluating the appropriateness of a definition. There are many definitions available for many words. The debater needs to neutralize the subjectivity of judges as much as possible by persuading them that standards of evaluation can determine the appropriate definition for the debate. We have identified the principal standards for definitions and their underlying rationale: grammatical context, each word should have meaning, reasonability, better definition, and debatability. Debaters should understand these general principles in order to understand the topicality argument.

Third, debaters must be able to apply topicality arguments appropriately. Debaters must apply definitions to cases and explain how definitions support the position that the case is or is not topical. Debaters must apply standards to definitions, explaining how the definition they defend meets the standard and how the definition they attack violates the standard. This skill is an important and difficult one to develop.

Fourth, clarity of presentation and resolution of arguments are critical to topicality arguments. Clarity and resolution are always important, but topicality is a semantic argument requiring the utmost precision and care in presentation. An argument about language, delivered under the pressure of a timed speech, can be very difficult to resolve. But if the debaters do not resolve it, the judge has no choice but to make a subjective evaluation. There is little the debater can offer in the way of objective evidence to support a topicality argument. The ability to persuade the judge hinges on fair standards and definitions, appropriately applied and compared.

Exercises

1. Assume your opponent is defending the resolution, "Resolved: that U.S. higher education has sacrificed quality for institutional survival." The opposition argues that high schools average too many students per classroom to effectively teach the subject matter. Identify the implicit definitions of the key terms of the resolution. How is your opponent defining "higher education," "quality," and "institutional survival?"

2. Define "freedom of speech" using a general dictionary, a specialty dictionary, legislative history, and an academic book or article. How are the definitions similar and how are they different? What does the comparison tell you about the biases of your sources?

3. Suppose you had two definitions for the term "arm sales" in the resolution, "Resolved: that the United States' arms sales are detrimental to the nation's long-term interests." Government sources define the term to mean any sale of weaponry constituting more than $7 to a foreign country. The other definition, from an academic source, argues that arms sales are the commerce of all weapons and spare parts used in the operation of those weapons. Defend each definition as a superior interpretation. Use the standards of definition identified in this chapter to fortify your arguments.

4. Assume you are advocating the resolution, "Resolved: that compulsory national service for all qualified U.S. citizens is desirable." Suppose your justification for affirming the resolution is that the nation could benefit from improved roadways, less trash on the nation's highways, etc. Defend that your interpretation of the resolution as viable. What definitions would you use? How does your defense of the resolution meet those definitions? Could you defend your definitions according to one of the standards we discuss in this chapter?

5. Suppose the resolution that you are debating against is "Resolved: that legal protection of accused persons in the United States unnecessarily hinders law enforcement agencies." Your opponent offers only one example of where the resolution appears to be true: they argue that the Guilty but Mentally Ill defense means that many guilty defendants have to serve little to no time in jail. Can you argue that this is a hasty generalization? How would you do it?

3

Analyzing Criteria Through Lines of Argument

Chapter Outline

Key Terms

criteria
value criteria
countercriteria
value hierarchy
value utility
value translation
value context

Jane: I think the dean ought to ban all offensive signs and paraphernalia that insult ethnic groups and women.

Maury: You know I don't like any of that stuff, but people have a right to free speech, even on campus.

Jane: But if you allow racial and sexual harassment, you leave students vulnerable to insults and injuries. You give the university a bad reputation, and you increase the risk of confrontation.

Maury: You cannot keep people from speaking their minds simply because you disagree with them. Telling people what is politically acceptable is tyrannical. Don't tell people what is right or wrong—let them learn through their own experiences.

Can Maury and Jane ever agree in this situation? Is it possible to compare the protection of individuals from sexist and racist harassment with the right to speak? Or are these two concerns irreconcilable? Conflicts between two opposing values occur regularly in value debate. If one debater continues to defend the importance of one value and the opponent merely supports a contrary value, the debate will degenerate into "two ships passing in the night."

Values cannot be expressed in a vacuum. Value conflicts occur because humans must forego some values in order to affirm others. By asserting that something is desirable, we imply that the absence of that value is undesirable. When values come into conflict, human beings need to have some system for determining which values they prefer.

Given that values will always conflict, debaters have an obligation to look for ways to reconcile opposing viewpoints. In the previous chapter, we examined standards for assessing competing definitions of resolutional terms. Here, we will look at means for determining the importance assigned to the values in a debate, which we will refer to as **criteria.** Criteria provide judges with a method for evaluating competing value arguments. Which values are better? When values compete, which deserve priority? Are some values more appropriate in certain circumstances than others?

Both affirmative and negative debaters can set up value criteria for evaluating their debates. Regardless of which side initiates the argument, the substance of the criteria remains the same. For labeling purposes in academic debate, affirmatives refer to their means of evaluation as **value criteria**, while negatives call their argument **countercriteria**. For the ease of our discussion, we will refer to all criteria arguments as simply value criteria.

Failure to establish criteria leaves open the question of how the judge should resolve value conflicts. Just as you find yourself at a strategic disadvantage if you allow your opponent to establish standards for definitions, you will hurt your chances by ignoring standards for evaluating value conflicts. By establishing criteria, you decrease the subjectivity of the judge's assessments and gain influence over the judge's conclusions. If you are fortunate enough to have an opponent who concedes your criteria, you should be in a position to win the value conflict.

After all, defining the rules of the game enhances your ability to control the outcome of the debate.

To establish value criteria, you must understand the options for evaluating conflicting values, recognize the circumstances that are appropriate for making specific criteria claims, and be able to argue why your criteria would be superior to any countercriteria presented in the debate. To show that your criteria are superior, you need to be able to explain the strengths of your own criteria and expose the weaknesses of your opponent's criteria.

Borrowing from the means for evaluating conflicting values in the public arena, we will identify four ways to compare arguments about values: value hierarchy, value utility, value translation, and value context. In each instance, we will define the strategy, explore the types of resolutions most appropriate for these criteria, and identify the strengths and weaknesses of the approaches. We will conclude the chapter with a discussion of how debaters can resolve value conflicts for a judge. This section will show how the ideas in the first portion of the chapter might function in a debate round.

Value Hierarchy

Each of us considers some values to be more important than others. When buying a car, you might want both economy and attractiveness from your purchase. Faced with a substantially cheaper economy car versus the sleek, sporty expensive model, you must make a choice. What's more important? Attractiveness or cash? To decide, you must rely on your own value hierarchy.

A **value hierarchy** is the prioritization of some values over others. Values are not equal. Some values are more central to individuals, while others have only a minimal importance. Western culture is filled with examples of value hierarchy. The Ten Commandments and the Golden Rule both represent examples of value hierarchy. The U.S. Constitution represents the binding law in the United States. The values enumerated in the Constitution and the Bill of Rights represent the highest values in U.S. law.

In the argument that opened this chapter, Jane and Maury can use value hierarchy to resolve their disagreement about free speech and harassment of minorities and women.

> Jane: Safety should be the number one priority of a university administration. If t-shirts, posters, and newsletters incite harassment, we have a responsibility to control such paraphernalia. We must protect the student first.

Jane's argument is that a hierarchy should place one value (physical safety) as a higher-order value than another (freedom of speech). Jane contends that there is a reason to make protection a higher-order value. By viewing the conflict from the administration's perspective, the physical well-being of the student is the university's highest liability. Liberty is important, but not at the expense of the students' safety.

Resolutional Application

Some debate resolutions are more appropriate for establishing value hierarchies than others. If the resolution explicitly states that one value is more important than another, it invites the use of the value-hierarchy criterion. Therefore, debaters on both sides of the question will want to consider the hierarchy embodied in the resolution as the standard to evaluate the arguments presented in the debate. Examine the following resolutions used previously for value debate:

> Resolved: that protection of the natural environment is a more important goal than the satisfaction of American energy demands.
> Resolved: that individual rights of privacy are more important than any other constitutional right.
> Resolved: that significantly stronger third-party participation in the U.S. presidential elections would benefit the political process.

In each of these resolutions, it is the explicit wording of the statement that suggests value hierarchy as an appropriate criterion. One value is explicitly stated as more important than another in the first two topics. The value of third-party participation is explicitly stated as more beneficial for the political process than the current two-party system.

Other resolutions invite the use of value hierarchy in an implicit manner. Here, the statements do not identify the two values along the hierarchy. Instead, the resolutions specify only one value as the focus of the debate.

> Resolved: that increased restrictions on civilian possession of handguns in the United States are justified.
>
> Resolved: that continued U.S. covert involvement in Central America would be undesirable.
>
> Resolved: that the American judicial system has overemphasized freedom of speech.

With only one value specified, debaters can discover conflicting values by searching the relevant literature on the subject. Regardless of which value the literature chooses to contrast with the explicit value, value hierarchy allows for a clear comparison between the two.

Strengths of Value Hierarchy

Perhaps the most appealing benefit of using a value hierarchy is its simplicity. Value hierarchies clearly identify which issues are more or less important in the debate. If debaters can maximize a higher-order value, they should win the debate. If they focus on a lower-order value, their arguments become irrelevant in the judge's evaluation.

> Jane: Universities can't be concerned with the free speech rights of a few students when lives are at stake. Physical safety of the students is clearly more important.

If Maury allows Jane's hierarchy to provide a framework for their conversation, he will likely lose the argument. Jane's statement that lives are more important to the university makes his argument less valuable by comparison.

A related benefit of value hierarchy is that it makes potential arguments very predictable for debater preparation. If you can defend your values as the most important consideration, contrasting values (whatever they may be) are less important. This advantage to debaters cannot be overstated. Regardless of what your opponent might choose to defend, you can anticipate that you will be able to argue that your value merits greater support. As a result, you can anticipate and prepare to make these comparisons in any debate on the topic.

> Jane: Protecting students has to be our number one priority. Freedom of speech, freedom of assembly, and freedom of the press are all valuable goals, but never at the expense of students' lives.

With this argument, Jane admits that Maury can identify several reasons to protect the words and actions of racists and sexists. Nevertheless, she defends that her value is more important in each case.

Weaknesses of Value Hierarchy

While appropriate in some instances, value hierarchy is vulnerable to several lines of attack. Applied too rigidly, value hierarchies can lead to absurd conclusions. This criterion assumes that a single hierarchy is applicable in all circumstances. You might desire a stable economy, but it is doubtful that you would support the reinstitution of slavery to achieve that end. Value hierarchies vary from context to context, so a strict adherence to one may be unpersuasive. Returning to our debate between Jane and Maury:

> Maury: Protecting the public from harm is an important goal, but it hardly justifies abridging speech. Would you be willing to sacrifice the freedom of speech for all Americans to save one life? Would you have stopped the American Revolution because soldiers died fighting for freedom of speech? There is a point at which you have to risk personal injury for free speech.

Maury's argument exposes the flaw of a rigid application of a value hierarchy. In certain contexts, human beings sacrifice a small amount of something important in order to secure larger amounts of a less valuable end. People consider wars to be the ultimate sacrifice because they surrender human life for the preservation of a state and its values. When applied without any consideration of context, then, a value hierarchy loses its persuasive force.

A second problem with value hierarchies is that they ignore the probabilistic nature of most arguments. They assume a certainty of outcomes; they do not take into account that values have varying probabilities of coming into existence. The assumption of certainty explains why those making religious arguments find hierarchies so persuasive. Based on faith, which is perhaps the most unshakable of all assumptions, those making religious arguments frequently believe that one value precedes another in importance. In questions of social science, politics, the law, and other secular concerns, however, value hierarchies may not be as persuasive.

> Maury: Schools should not sacrifice free speech to protect female and minority students. We can't be sure that any student's life will be in danger, but we know that suppressing speech will affect everyone on campus.

In this example, Maury introduces the probabilities affecting the two values in the decision. He feels that the loss of free speech is a certain consequence of adhering to the uncertainty of protecting students from injury. Rigid application of a value structure when outcomes are uncertain may lead to costly errors. Even those who believe free speech is less important might believe that a definitive loss of free speech should be protected against the uncertain consequences of allowing it to occur.

A third problem with value hierarchies in debate is that they are susceptible to cooptation by the other team. Hierarchies establish which value should be more important; they do not specify whether the affirmative or the negative comes closer to the higher-order value. Suppose, for example, that Jane had firmly established safety as a more important concern along a hierarchy. If Maury could come up with an argument to demonstrate that his position actually achieves greater safety, Jane would be, in effect, trapped by her hierarchy.

> Maury: It is also possible that by protecting free speech, you may actually decrease injury to people. By allowing these frustrated racists and sexists to let off a little steam verbally, perhaps we will decrease the physical conflicts.

Maury argues that allowing free speech is the best way to achieve the goal that Jane advocates—freedom from physical injury. He maintains that free speech functions as a safety valve for those unable to achieve their goals in other ways. His position becomes the means to maximize Jane's value. As a result, Maury's value becomes more persuasive because of Jane's own hierarchy.

A value hierarchy is a rigid criterion that distinguishes higher-order values from lower-order ones. The value hierarchy is very appropriate for resolutions that explicitly or implicitly argue the comparative worth of two values. Despite its simplicity and predictability, debaters should be aware of the weaknesses of hierarchies. They should use the criterion when it is resolutionally appropriate, when the criterion has some universal support, when the outcome of advocacy is relatively certain, and when competing arguments cannot maximize higher-order values.

Value Utility

Rather than argue that one value is more important than another on an abstract scale, **value utility** argues that the preferred value should be the one that provides the greatest good to the greatest number of people. If you have several brothers and sisters, your parents probably used value utility to determine where to send you to school. If they had limited financial resources, they might have sent each of your siblings to a public institution. They might have opted out of sending only one child to private school because they received more utility by providing educations for your entire family.

The criterion of value utility is pervasive in American society. Republicans generally argue the importance of volunteerism to help the poor, maintaining that fewer governmental programs would focus charity on those who need help. Democrats usually respond that governmental programs are necessary to ensure that all of those who are poor receive help. Both parties argue that utility of their approaches should mean that they be used to solve the problem of poverty in the United States.

The concept of reducing values to their most utilitarian form is appealing. Such a strategy allows the debate to shift from abstract calculations of values to direct comparison of effects. The debater who can defend the method most useful in achieving an important result will likely control the debate.

> Jane: A campus needs harmony to function as an educational and social environment. People who cause trouble with personal attacks on women and ethnic groups should be suspended or expelled in order to ensure the right

environment for the campus. The free speech of a few cannot justify disruption of the entire campus, no more than the right to yell fire in a crowded theater can threaten the peace of the public.

Jane argues that preserving the harmony of the whole campus is far more important than the free speech of a few individuals. Jane's argument is that the utility to the campus, a social and learning environment, would be seriously disrupted by allowing social discord generated by flagrant demonstrations of racism and sexism. By reducing the value conflict to a utilitarian calculus, Jane is attempting to persuade Maury that the campus as a whole would be better if the school tolerated a small infringement on the rights of a few individuals.

Resolutional Application

Some debate resolutions clearly lend themselves to a utilitarian calculus. Resolutions that define how a value should be affirmed (frequently called quasi-policy resolutions) are usually well suited for a criterion of utility. These resolutions describe specific objectives needed in society. Consider the following examples:

> Resolved: that increased restrictions on civilian possession of handguns in the United States is justified.
> Resolved: that the trend toward increasing foreign investment in the United States is detrimental to the nation.
> Resolved: that a unilateral freeze by the United States on nuclear weapons production and development would be desirable.

In each of these examples, the statements specify a means that would yield a desirable or undesirable end. The focus on means invites the use of a utilitarian criterion to resolve conflicting value claims.

A second type of resolution appropriate to the use of value utility is one that implicates one value as the means to the achievement of another explicitly stated value. While similar to the previous examples useful for this criterion, these resolutions explicitly state both the means and ends that should be the focus of the discussion.

> Resolved: that significantly stronger third-party participation in the U.S. Presidential elections would benefit the political process.
> Resolved: that regulations in the United States requiring employees to be tested for controlled substances are an unwarranted invasion of privacy.
> Resolved: that activism in politics by religious groups harms the American political process.

Each of these resolutions examines the relationship between some specified means and some specified end. They can be analyzed through value utility because the goals expressed bear an instrumental relationship to one another.

Finally, the subject matter embodied in some resolutions invites the value-utility criterion. The wording of the resolution is not the focus here. But when the debater begins to research the subject area of the resolution, the relevant literature will suggest assessments based on utility.

> Resolved: that membership in the United Nations is no longer beneficial to the United States.
> Resolved: that the American judicial system has overemphasized freedom of the press.
> Resolved: that compulsory national service for all qualified U.S. citizens is desirable.

None of the resolutions explicitly indicates the use of value utility. Nevertheless, the literature explaining why the United States should no longer belong to the United Nations, why the judicial system has overemphasized freedom of the press, and why compulsory national service would be desirable will likely focus on the utility of these specified means. Or, at least, the literature will examine the relationship between these means and particular outcomes.

Through subject matter and wording, some resolutions suggest value utility as a criterion to determine the probable truth of the resolution. However, that does not mean that debaters cannot use other criteria if they can justify their alternative choices. It is possible that after establishing the utility of using one value as a means of achieving another, debaters will need to compare the final outcomes posed by each scenario.

Strengths of Value Utility

Value utility can be beneficial to debaters because it allows a debater to use one value to maximize others. If one value becomes the means to achieving another, its own importance is more significant.

> Jane: If the school prevents students from engaging in harassing forms of speech, it will send a message that racist and sexist remarks are intolerable. If the students get that message consistently, society would become a lot more tolerant and we would have a lot less hate crime.

Here, Jane broadens the value of preventing harassing speech. She describes the decision to block this type of speech as the means to achieving the goal of a more tolerant society. If society becomes more tolerant, the number of hate crimes will diminish. By using value utility, then, she elevates the problem from one of harassment to one of violence in society.

The second benefit of using value utility is that the criterion allows the debaters to measure the implications of a given value. Values can be amorphous, creating difficulty for the debater attempting to prove something is necessary or beneficial. Value utility remedies this problem by discussing the probability of one value affecting another. It concerns itself with the degree of one value that must be present to ensure an impact on another.

Jane: Only a handful of students want to exercise their "right" to harass others. By refusing to allow them to do so, we remove a negative experience for all minorities and women on campus.

In this example, Jane assesses the comparative utility of the competing values in her conflict with Maury. Only a small number of students want to use their freedom of speech to harass other students. One racist poster or one sexist sweatshirt can have stressful implications for all women and minorities on the campus. Jane argues that more students benefit from a ban on harassing speech than lose their exercise of offensive speech. The optimal utility, Jane would argue, clearly rests with preventing the exercise of speech by a few in order to decrease stress on many.

Weaknesses of Value Utility

One of the first problems associated with a criterion of utility is that it depends on the success of proving that the value is capable of achieving an ideal end state. This can be difficult because a multitude of factors could intervene, making the ultimate goal extremely difficult to reach.

Initially, this problem lies in determining when to apply the instrumental value. Arguing that a given goal can be achieved through the agency of another begs the question of deciding if that value needs to be applied in order to solve the problem. Since many means can achieve a given end, we cannot be certain that the value being defended is the best alternative. Either the problem may not yet exist, or it may not be sufficiently severe to warrant the imposition of the values in question.

Maury: Jane, you can't know if and when the campus will erupt because of these sexist and racist signs. You shouldn't say we should compromise free speech when we don't know whether there will be a problem.

Maury argues that Jane cannot justify the means of restricting speech if she cannot prove that the threat of disruption from the exercise of speech will become a reality.

Even debaters who can answer this sort of question are not off the hook. They must also be able to show that the instrumental value will achieve the required goals. Consider this argument from Maury:

Maury: We have absolutely no assurance that banning sexist and racist *expression* will make any dent in sexism and racism. People could become more dangerously sexist and racist when they are forced to take their opinions underground.

Here he is questioning the utility of the restriction toward the goal of protecting the learning environment. If the utility of restricting free speech is not clearly proven, then it is difficult to warrant its selection over other competing choices.

A second problem associated with value utility is that it may not be sufficient to warrant the acceptance of a value. One value may be the means to achieving another, but at some point, the relationship between the end and other competing interests becomes important. In other words, it is not enough to show instrumental relationships. Debaters must also be able to defend the intrinsic worthiness of their positions.

> Maury: I'm not sure that preservation of order on campus is worth compromising free speech. Even if campus order would be preserved, it sure seems to me that social disorder is the price we pay to protect the Bill of Rights.

Maury argues that the preservation of order on campus is not worth the price paid in the loss of free speech. In this way, he suggests that despite the importance of social order, free speech should not be sacrificed to achieve it.

The final problem with value utility is that it does not exclude the possibility that a competing value may meet the criteria more fully. A competing value can be a more effective means for achieving the ideal end state than the original claim.

> Maury: Maybe you're right that we should preserve campus order. But if you keep people from expressing themselves, you may create an undercurrent of discontent that could explode. Perhaps the best route to order is through free speech.

Maury insists that the ultimate goal of protecting minorities and women is to prevent campus-wide discord. The best way to maximize that concern is to guarantee free expression. Free speech, he reasons, allows society's malcontents to voice their frustrations verbally rather than physically. This "safety valve" argument maximizes Jane's criterion of preserving campus order.

Value Translation

Sometimes, the best way to resolve value conflicts is to translate the competing concerns into some common objective—**value translation.** When looking for a potential home, two parents could have a disagreement. One parent could want to purchase an inexpensive property, while the other seeks a home in an upscale neighborhood. After some discussion, they might realize that what they both really want is a quality education for their children. The first parent wants to save money on a house payment to increase their educational savings fund. The second parent wants a better neighborhood to improve the chances that the children will receive a better education. Translating their values in this manner, they can resolve their differences by determining which strategy will better serve their long-term educational goals.

Value translation is frequently used to resolve value conflicts that occur in nonacademic debate settings. When legislators have to decide issues of environmental protection and land development, they regularly use cost-benefit analysis. Cost-benefit analysis is a form of value translation. How do you compare jobs from development with protection of the environment? Within the framework of cost-benefit analysis, legislators might assign a monetary value to both the potential jobs from development and the potential consequences to the environment.

CRITERIA ARGUMENT

In the final round of the 1989 Cross-Examination Debate Association National Championships, Gonzaga University (William DeForest and Dave Hanson) affirmed the resolution, "Resolved: that increased restrictions on the civilian possession of handguns in the United States are justified." Southern Illinois University (John Lapham and Mark West) negated the resolution. Mr. DeForest presented the criteria for Gonzaga, emphasizing the criteria of *value translation*. Mr. Lapham offered the negative response.

First Affirmative

We offer this test in observation one, resolutional criteria. Deciding whether increased restrictions would be justified involves the application of a two-level test. A. The scope of Second Amendment freedoms is the proper question. Visiting scholar at Harvard Law School Joyce Malcolm notes the significance of the Second Amendment's interpretation in the debate on handgun restrictions in 1983. "Nearly all writers agree . . . that an accurate reading of the Second Amendment is indispensable to resolving current debates over gun ownership." In order to be justified, handgun restrictions must be deemed permissible with respect to this amendment. Maynard Jackson, former mayor of Atlanta, notes in 1977: "Central to the [gun control] issue, of course, is interpretation of the Second Amendment to the United States Constitution. That Amendment reads as follows: A well-regulated militia, being necessary to the security of a free State, the right of the people to keep and bear arms, shall not be infringed. The amendment is the beginning and the end of any discussion of the legal merits of gun control." The reason for this designation is relatively simple. Poorly drafted laws may violate constitutional freedoms other than the Second Amendment. For example, requiring summary execution for the possession

First Negative

On observation number one, on the A Subpoint. The first two cards are perfect. They indicate that the debate over the gun control issue begins and ends at the Second Amendment, and Mark and I would agree.

My second response, though, is that we will object to the value. . . . [Justifying gun control by using the Second Amendment as criterion is inherently patriarchal. By defending gun control on the basis of the laws in the society, the affirmative reinforces the dictates pronounced by a patriarchal society.]

The third response is this gives a deeper analysis into the basis of law, and it allows you to look beyond just the term to what the term connotes.

The final response to the A Subpoint is that their criteria tell you to think in legal ways, but we would indicate that is bad.

B Subpoint says compelling interest. First we would ask you to allow value objections to their criteria on the training responses even though their criterion is rational basis.

(Continued)

CRITERIA ARGUMENT—Continued

First Affirmative (Cont.)

of a Saturday night special would violate Eighth Amendment protections against cruel and unusual punishment. However, the unjustified portion of the law would be its enforcement, not the restriction on Saturday night specials per se. The application of the Second Amendment, along with analogous State-granted rights, are therefore the relevant legal questions regarding the restrictions themselves.

Their application is discussed in B. Compelling interest and rational basis are the proper tests.

The Constitution protects two types of liberties: fundamental and nonfundamental rights. The test of any restriction which infringes on a fundamental right is whether or not a compelling interest in public safety or welfare, or a genuine advantage is accrued by law. Restrictions which infringe on nonfundamental rights, however, must only show that the legislature had a rational basis for passing the restriction. Law professors Nowak, Rotunda, and Young explain in their 1986 constitutional law text. "Whenever fundamental rights are limited, the laws will have to promote an overriding or compelling interest of government in order to be valid. . . . When the governmental action relates only to matters of economics or general social welfare, the law need only rationally relate to a legitimate governmental purpose."

C. Judicial precedent regarding the Second Amendment has presumptive value. There are several reasons why a judicial precedent, once established,

First Negative (Cont.)

The second response [to] the resolutional question is that you the panel, and not necessarily the courts, are to decide whether or not the increased restrictions are justified.

The third response is that the affirmative would change the resolutional question. They would have you ask whether or not the courts would adopt the restrictions. But, clearly, you have been asked to decide that, not the courts. We would indicate that an improper focus would be given this way.

The next response, we would indicate that you should adopt an active judging role. And that is that if you adopt the rational basis criteria, then you decide whether or not you think it's rational to vote for the affirmative. Do not simply rubber stamp what the affirmative tells you that the courts would do.

The next response is that we would indicate that if you accept it, you should take it yourself and use it as a filter, or if you see a disadvantage to their case, you would not see it rational, you would see it irrational to vote for the affirmative under this basis.

The final response is we would indicate that the dialectic between the teams requires more than you simply line up law journals and cite cases. We think you should look beyond intent to what actually

(Continued)

CRITERIA ARGUMENT—*Continued*

First Affirmative (Cont.)

should be followed. These include fairness, legitimacy of the law, and the credibility of the court system. As a result, while precedents are overruled on occasion, those occasions are rare. Law Professors Murphy, Fleming, and Harris agree in their 86 law text. "In fact, of course, a tribunal that frequently reversed itself could not expect others to respect its decisions. Not surprisingly, then, stare decisis is the normal guide even in the Supreme Court. Overrulings come, but they come infrequently."

Of course, the courts have ruled on many gun restrictions before. In fact, these rulings have remained highly consistent. Thus, while we certainly acknowledge that courts are fallible, the values inherent in adhering to precedent as a guide to interpretation grant it presumptive value, even to we nonjudicial actors. Paul Colby, assistant U.S. attorney for the DC district, argues in 1987. "The rules binding lower courts to adhere to precedent are, therefore, not compulsory but suasive, as they are with respect to nonjudicial actors."

Thus, while court precedent is clearly not absolute, a compelling procedural reason must be provided in order to depart from judicial precedent regarding the Second Amendment's interpretation. Please note that this is not an independent criteria, it is only one means by which you might meet the rational basis test.

First Negative (Cont.)

happened. Princeton Political [Science] professor David Nadelman argues in 1989 that when laws depend on a certain moral they can inflict great moral damage on innocent parties; we must rethink our moral position.

C Subpoint says that precedent equals value. My first response is that these are often ignored. Joseph Brandies argues in 1924 that "Stare Decisis is ordinarily a wise rule of action, but it is not a universal inexorable command. The instances to which the court has disregarded the admonition are many."

My next response is, that would be a turn around. And that would be that the disutility of the precedent requires its rejection. The Boston University Law Review reported in 1986 that "Stare Decisis has long been seen as one of the great neutral principals of legal analysis. In truth, it is nothing but the rhetorical ally of those in favor of yesterdays decisions. The world of constitutional adjudication would be well served by a rejection of this doctrine" But we would indicate that you decrease debate by simply citing precedent.

A variety of factors, including prospective tourism, the worth of natural resources, and the attractiveness of the area for other forms of investment, could serve as the basis for judging the monetary value of the environment. The legislators would then compare this dollar figure to the prospective value in jobs and taxes from investment. By translating all of these inputs into two monetary figures, planners can assess the costs and benefits of investment compared to environmental regulation.

Value translation shares with value utility the characteristics of seeking to maximize one value by supporting or upholding others. Where it differs is that translation requires that the ultimate objective of both values be the same. Through this process, translation permits debaters to transform two divergent values into one common entity that allows for a direct comparison.

> Jane: Maury, you say that free speech is important. But why? Is it because speech provides a means for those oppressed to force the evolution of society? If that is so, then suppressing reactionary speech is a wiser course to sustain social advances.

With this argument, Jane establishes social evolution as the common objective of both free speech and regulation of harassing speech. Having determined the common end, she maintains by regulating speech offensive to minorities and women, we are more likely to achieve social progress.

Resolutional Application

Some debate resolutions suggest translation as an appropriate criterion for evaluating disputes about values. Resolutions that assert *how* one value should be preferred over another are appropriate for such translation.

> Resolved: that the rights of the accused are more important than the
> freedom of the press.
> Resolved: that American TV has sacrificed quality for entertainment.
> Resolved: that protection of the national environment is a more
> important goal than the satisfaction of America's energy demands.

Each one of these resolutions provides a framework for value translation. In the first, both free press and the rights of the accused can be translated into justice. For the second, quality and entertainment of television might both serve the end of educating the public. In the final example, the nation's environment and satisfaction of energy demands both contribute to the ultimate goal of a higher standard of living.

Resolutions that suggest how a value should be achieved also indicate value translation as a comparative tool. These resolutions are sometimes referred to as quasi-policy resolutions because they isolate values implicit in competing policy directives.

> Resolved: that activism in politics by religious groups harms the
> American political process.
> Resolved: that government censorship of public artistic expression in the
> United States is an undesirable infringement on individual rights.

Again, these resolutions allow translation into a common goal. Political activism by religious groups and improvement of the political process both aim to broaden political participation overall. Censorship and individual liberties both attempt to protect the individual.

Strengths of Value Translation

Value translation results in a broad-based appeal that diminishes the risks of judge bias against a particular value. Even if the judge supports your opponent's value, translation permits you to elevate the discussion to a common goal. This process co-opts the judge's allegiance to your opponent's value and shifts the focus of the debate to who better maximizes the common value.

> Jane: I recognize that most people would prefer to protect free speech rather than
> to restrict it for the safety of a few individuals. But if social advancement is the
> rationale for protecting speech, that goal can more easily be achieved by
> restricting offensive speech.

Jane is sensitive enough to realize that opposing free speech is ordinarily not a very persuasive stance. She improves her chances of winning the argument by shifting the discussion away from the unpopular effect of her proposal and onto the shared objective of both approaches.

Value translation is also beneficial to debaters because it provides a means of direct comparison. Rather than trying to determine which value is more important, it redefines all the issues in the debate to a common set of terms. This simplifies the debate, allowing the debaters to focus on the probability that a given value or countervalue will achieve the shared objective. Rather than being a debate between free speech and harassment of minorities and women, value translation gives Maury and Jane an opportunity to discuss all their arguments in terms of their impact on social advancement.

Weaknesses of Value Translation

One of the biggest dangers in value translation is that you may not be able to persuade the judge that your option maximizes the common goal. Your opponent's argument might have a more direct relationship with the encompassing value.

> Maury: What made the civil rights movement possible was free speech. The
> movement was successful because more speech is the antidote to bad speech.
> The civil rights movement and the women's movement defeated bigotry on
> the rhetorical battlefield because the movements were correct. They will defeat

the rhetoric of bigotry whenever there is a level playing field because false ideas die when exposed to the truth.

Maury argues that rather than aid the civil rights movement as Jane suggests, banning free speech may hurt civil rights. He argues that exposing the false ideas of bigotry to public debate weakens the position of the bigot. When speech is free, he suggests, truth will defeat ignorance. A weakness of translation, then, is the potential that a given means may fail to maximize the common objective.

A second problem with value translation is that the common objective sought does not necessarily represent preeminent values. Even if the affirmative can maximize a common goal, the negative debater may choose to defend another value as more important.

> Maury: Even if allowing harassing speech were to damage the civil rights movement, I believe we must still tolerate it. Free speech is too important to be sacrificed on the altar of one social movement.

Maury argues that the value of free speech does not rest on what it accomplishes, even if it aids a movement he finds worthy of protection. The value of free speech lies within itself. With this position, Maury is attempting to establish a value hierarchy with free speech as the preeminent value. Debaters need to be aware that merely maximizing a common goal does not necessarily persuade the judge to support their side of the question.

Another difficulty with value translation is that not all values can be translated. Take the resolution, "Resolved: that increased restrictions on civilian possession of handguns in the United States would be justified." An affirmative debater might claim that the restrictions are necessary to reduce the number of accidental deaths from guns. A negative debater would argue that individual liberty should come first. Translating these two values would be difficult. It is hard to imagine a common goal possible from protecting an individual's liberty and accidental gun deaths. One improves the quality of life; the other increases the possibility of life without concern for its quality.

In sum: value translation can be a particularly useful criterion when the resolution suggests two values that must compete and when the resolution suggests how to achieve a value. Translation can be a strategically powerful argumentation method. It reduces judge bias about competing values and it allows for direct comparison. However, it also suffers from some weaknesses. Value translation does not avoid the problem of probabilistic claims or hierarchies that can dispute the merits of the common concern. Also, some notions may be difficult to translate into more common values.

Value Context

The context of a value conflict is an important element for determining whether one idea is more important than another. You might think that the nation should have a free press, but should newspapers be able to report on the exact location of our armed forces in a military conflict? Should they be able to report the names of rape victims or children molested by their parents? **Value context** is a standard that relies on specific circumstances to assess the importance of value.

The U.S. Constitution contains many values that are generally considered to be absolute guiding principles for the nation. Nevertheless, instances arise that require the Supreme Court to compromise these values in particular circumstances. The prohibition against yelling fire in a crowded theater is an exception to free speech protection; press coverage that endangers national security is an exception to free press protection. Debaters should be alert to particularized circumstances that might suggest exceptions to absolute interpretations of values.

Jane and Maury have numerous opportunities to employ contextual criteria in their debate about free speech on campus.

> Jane: I agree that free speech is generally an important value. However, some values have to be compromised in certain circumstances. A school cannot afford to have its name embarrassed by the ravings of a small ignorant minority! The integrity of the school is at stake and can be easily damaged by bad publicity about a few individuals.

Here, Jane admits that free speech might be a higher value than freedom from harassment. However, she also argues that in the context of an institution of learning, the incidents spawned by harassment will injure the reputation of the university. Jane concedes that free speech might be more important generally, but in this context, the integrity of the learning institution is more important.

Value context is sometimes referred to as a kind of "situational" ethic, or "relative" morality. Do not be surprised if you hear these labels applied in either debates or casual conversation. Debaters who plan to defend value context should be familiar with attacks on situational ethics. Those who choose to attack context should be aware of its strengths.

Resolutional Application

Debaters should analyze many resolutions in relationship to their specific contexts. Sometimes, resolutions will specify the context a judge should use to evaluate a given value.

> Resolved: that U.S. higher education has sacrificed quality for institutional survival.
> Resolved: that violence is a justified response to political pressure.
> Resolved: that activism in politics by religious groups harms the American political process.

Each of these resolutions identifies the context that the judge should use when assessing the value. Affirmative debaters must argue that higher education has sacrificed quality for institutional survival, and not for other reasons. Violence is a justified response to political pressures, and not to other pressures. Activism by religious groups harms the American political process, making other potential benefits of the groups irrelevant.

Some topics imply that particular circumstances justify affirming a value that might otherwise be questionable. Exceptions exist to some generally accepted principles. These resolutions narrow the framework of the value's impact.

> Resolved: that the federal government should grant amnesty to all those who evaded the draft during the Vietnam War.
>
> Resolved: that a U.S. foreign policy significantly directed toward the furtherance of human rights is desirable.
>
> Resolved: that significant government restrictions on coverage by U.S. media of terrorist activity are justified.

None of these resolutions excludes broader interpretations of the value. But at a minimum, the affirmative needs to address the Vietnam-era draft evaders, the human rights aspects of foreign policy of the United States, and media coverage of terrorist activities. Perhaps draft evaders should be prosecuted and perhaps the media should not be censored, but in the case of the Vietnam War and in the case of terrorism, exceptions can be made. While all foreign policy should not be controlled by human rights concerns, in some circumstances, human rights should be furthered.

Strengths of Value Context

Value context is useful to debaters because it places claims about the benefits or consequences of a value in perspective. It prevents overclaiming an argument to such a degree that an absurd conclusion results.

> Jane: I do not believe harassing speech merits the same protection as the speech protected by the Constitution, namely, the right to protest actions of the government. There are a few isolated individuals harassing normal students on our campus. There is no free speech interest here. To protect students from slanderous racial remarks, we have to see that some rights are, at times, more important than free speech.

Here, Jane argues that not to consider the circumstances in which the speech occurs devalues the protection of free speech. In this context, she reasons, the same rationale prompting the constitutional protection does not exist. The students are not challenging the government; they are merely attempting to harass their fellow students. Therefore, in this case, restrictions on free speech are warranted.

By reducing the possibility that debaters will take value claims to the extreme, value context provides a strong opportunity to present a persuasive case for an evaluative standard. Strong attention to the circumstances within which a value is operating exposes in-depth rationales for the appropriate consideration of values.

> Jane: Institutions have never recognized an absolute value to free speech. Editorialists of school newspapers have some restrictions on their speech for the very purpose that campus harmony must be in place for students to learn. Racist

and sexist language is just the sort of offensive speech that universities have traditionally restricted.

With this example, Jane makes a context-specific argument for insisting on campus speech restrictions. Within the university setting, she points to traditional restrictions on speech as a way of promoting campus harmony. The necessity of protecting the learning environment, she reasons, justifies a small infringement on an otherwise protected right.

The use of a criterion specific to the context can have strategic advantages in debate. If debaters can establish a narrow, clear, and definitive standard for determining the context of an exception, they can constrain the argumentative ground of the debate.

Weaknesses of Value Context

Despite its advantages, value context also has its drawbacks. The first line of argument used to undermine context is that criteria should not be based on circumstantial need.

> Maury: Free speech is fundamental whether it be in a schoolyard or in an outhouse. The place where the speech occurs does not justify its restriction. Freedom of speech is a fundamental right that we should not compromise in any forum.

In this example, Maury argues that there are some values in a hierarchy that decision makers should not compromise under any circumstances. History is replete with examples of individuals unwilling to compromise their beliefs. Sir Thomas More is often referred to as a man who was willing to die rather than to go against his religious beliefs. Patrick Henry is most famous for having uttered, "Give me liberty or give me death!" For a long time, humans have held that some absolute values are beyond compromise in any circumstances.

Another difficulty with value context is that a single exception can lead to other exceptions. In everyday life, this can lead to a loss of moral character as an individual struggles to do only what seems best at the moment. The use of context criteria can open a debater to the argument that there is not a defensible criterion if the judge resolves each debate based on context rather than moral principle.

> Maury: The problem with making exceptions is once they get started, there's no stopping them. Today we prohibit harassing speech, tomorrow we stop all speech we don't agree with. When we compromise a value once, we begin a long slide down a slippery slope to compromising all our freedoms.

Maury argues that Jane's willingness to compromise free speech in the case of racial and sexual epithets risks further loss of speech in other circumstances. This argument is sometimes referred to as the slippery slope argument in debates. Compromising a fundamental value leads to further compromises of that value.

A third problem with value context is that the criterion might not be appropriate to the context. Debaters can misjudge the critical elements of circumstances resulting in misleading conclusions about what the context requires.

> Maury: I do not believe the school's reputation can or will be hurt because of the aberrant behavior of a few individuals. Most schools in America have suffered some embarrassment like this in recent years. But people are not leaving these schools and alumni have not stopped supporting them. People know that these racists and sexists do not represent the views of the school.

Maury argues that Jane is overly concerned with the problem of reputation in the university context. Individuals who support the university realize that many diverse groups and opinions exist on campus, as they do elsewhere in society. The public will not judge a school by the unusual behavior of a few extremists. As a result, the college is unlikely to risk its good reputation.

The fourth problem of using value context is that your opponent may be able to maximize the value you identify as appropriate to the context.

> Maury: I would be far more concerned about the school becoming known for inhibiting free speech, encouraging political orthodoxy, and creating an environment where ideas are hidden rather than discussed in the open. The school's reputation as a forum for confronting and discovering ideas would be harmed far more if it inhibits the learning environment.

Even within the criterion established in this context, Maury argues that Jane may be incorrect. Instead of aiding the school's reputation, the restrictions on speech may erode the reputation of the school as a learning institution. Debaters must be careful that their opponents cannot maximize the value they are establishing as important in a particular context.

To summarize, some resolutions tend to invite value-context standards. Broadly worded resolutions or resolutions embodying exceptions may be difficult to defend without context-specific standards. When using this criterion, debaters need to be aware of the potential strengths and weaknesses of value contexts. Contexts allow debaters to avoid absurd conclusions, making it possible for debaters to present persuasive rationales for a particular form of evaluation. Nevertheless, value contexts may directly conflict with values established in a hierarchy. Context analysis may lead to a series of decisions compromising important concerns in a slow and gradual process. Finally, value contexts suffer from the ability of the opponent to maximize the value instead.

Resolving Conflicting Criteria

You have probably noticed by now that some resolutions lend themselves to more than one criterion. That is why, throughout this chapter, we have relied on the same resolution to illustrate statements that invite two or more types of criteria. Even if the resolutions do not explicitly call for conflicting criteria, debaters will frequently face opposing criteria in a debate. In these instances, they must be able to indicate why the criteria or criterion they defend is the strongest one presented. Debaters may use multiple criteria in any given debate, but the process of proving any one criterion superior to an opposing criterion is the same regardless of how many criteria are at issue in a round. For simplicity's sake, we will refer to resolving a single criterion against another.

The strength of a criterion results from two considerations: Which criterion is most relevant in the debate and which criterion is most meaningful for evaluating potential value conflicts. The remainder of this chapter, then, will address these two issues, providing several lines of argument that debaters can use to support their choices.

Is the Criterion Relevant to the Debate?

The relevance of a criterion for a given debate is not as simple as it appears at first glance. Debaters can argue about whether their own criterion and the criterion of their opponents are relevant to the resolution, to the value being affirmed, or to the value the negative is defending.

Criterion Not Relevant to the Resolution

At times, debaters may elect to argue that their opponent is not defending a criterion relevant to the resolution. Throughout this chapter, we have identified the types of resolutions that suggest particular types of criteria.

Value hierarchy is appropriate for resolutions that suggest that one value is more important than another. Value utility is appropriate for resolutions that suggest how a value should be affirmed. Value translation works with resolutions that explain how one value should be preferred over another or how a value should be affirmed. Value context is appropriate for resolutions that explicitly provide a context or suggest exceptions to a general value hierarchy. While some overlap exists, the phrasing of the resolution can often provide debaters with a rationale for arguing that a particular criterion is more appropriate.

Debaters should examine the wording of a resolution to see if the criterion that their opponent advocates fits with the resolution. If the criterion does not, they can persuasively argue that an alternative criterion would be more appropriate. If the opponents are incapable of defending that their criterion is the most appropriate for the resolution, it is doubtful that they will be able to convince the judge to affirm the resolution.

Criterion Not Relevant to the Value Affirmed

At times, debaters may attempt to use a criterion that is not relevant to the values affirmed by the resolution. The criterion may trivialize or elevate the values to unacceptable levels. In the resolution, "Resolved: that significantly stronger third-party participation in the U.S. presidential elections would benefit the political process," debaters may attempt to argue that third-party participation would help the environment or preserve world peace. These are certainly laudable values, but they must be defended specifically in the context of third-party participation. Debaters would have to show how both of these important values result from the "benefit[s]" of "the political process" achieved by third-party participation. Otherwise, the criterion that establishes these values as important would not have been shown to be relevant to the values embodied in the resolution.

Criterion Does Not Consider Competing Value Choices

Negative debaters are constantly seeking to identify the values that the resolution negates. Periodically, they discover that there are conflicting values the criteria in the debate do not take into account. When a criterion can be shown to ignore important competing values, it becomes highly suspect as a means of evaluating the resolution. Judges are unlikely to consider a criterion worthy if it systematically excludes important questions. Negative debaters can defeat an affirmative criterion if they can prove that it does not consider the implications of these other, perhaps more important, values.

> Maury: There is no way you can compare free speech with the reputation of the school. The school won't be damaged enough to justify a wholesale restriction on speech. Speech is very important and the consequence to a school's reputation over a single incident doesn't begin to compare.

Maury's argument is that Jane is not providing a sufficient criterion by arguing that the reputation of the school is important. It may be important on some occasions, but it is not important if schools would have to violate free speech in order to protect it. Negative debaters need to be very sensitive to the possibility that even their own criterion may not be encompassing enough to be relevant to the argument they are defending.

This principle can be applied to affirmative criteria that fail to filter negative criteria. In effect, such affirmative criteria provide no defense against a well-prepared negative. In the resolution, "Resolved: that the trend toward increasing foreign investment in the United States is detrimental to this nation," it is likely that an affirmative debater would establish the effect on U.S. economic stability as an appropriate criterion. While economic stability would be an important value in common circumstances, a negative team could argue that there are other values that render it a lower priority. The negative could argue that foreign investment fosters tense international relations by increasing hostility between American citizens fearful of increasing investment and foreign heads of state fearful of possible American backlash. The undercurrent of tension may lead to trade wars that culminate in military conflicts between nations. In this instance, the affirmative criterion (maximizing economic security) does not take into account the competing value offered by the negative (world peace). While economic stability might generally appear to be a goal worth attaining, few would do so at the expense of war.

Debaters can attack criteria for relevance to three arguments in a debate: relevance to the resolution, relevance to the affirmed values, and relevance to competing values. If they fail to prove the relevance of the criteria as a way of measuring any of these elements, they will probably not win the debate.

Is the Criterion Meaningful?

Debaters can establish a relevant criterion, but then fail to provide a criterion that has meaning within the context of the debate. They can argue that their opponent's criterion is meaningless by showing that it does not provide a workable measure of the value, that it is too narrow to be meaningful, or that it is too vague to be applicable.

Can the Criterion Measure the Value?

When attempting to evaluate whether to affirm a value, it becomes important to assess the importance of the value and other competing interests. This can be difficult, as some criteria do not lend themselves to definitive measurements. We might ask, for example, how much free speech would be damaged by restrictions on certain types of expression, or how significantly the privacy of a railroad engineer is curtailed by mandatory drug testing. In such instances, it becomes difficult to know how much of the value is necessary to produce a positive effect or how much effect affirming the value will have in a given set of circumstances. Without a clear criterion capable of measuring the outcome, opponents can argue that the benefits of conflicting values are also unknowable.

> Maury: We can't know how much a climate of racial hatred contributes to a chilling of free speech. Is one racist sign capable of instilling fear into those who would speak for racial equality? Or would thousands of t-shirts with racist slogans be necessary? The bottom line is we can't know because it's impossible to quantify the impact on free speech.

The problem can be, as Maury argues against Jane, that you might not be able to measure how much stronger the value becomes by affirming it. Affirmative debaters who establish a criterion should strive to show that there will be a quantifiable or qualitative impact by affirming the value in the resolution. Similarly, negative debaters should prepare to make the same judgments about their countercriterion.

Is the Criterion Broad Enough for Meaningful Application?

At times, debaters will be tempted to establish criteria so narrowly that it is difficult to meaningfully apply them to a conflict.

> Maury: Jane, you are right that sexist and racist language is wrong. The school should never condone this behavior; you are correct. However, there are other issues at stake and we have to consider all the interests, not merely whether something is right or wrong. We are a society that tolerates people's tendency to make mistakes.

Many of us have had discussions in which the moral criterion is so stringent that there is no room to question what is right or wrong. However, applying those standards to a value conflict does not always provide direction on how to resolve the problem. Maury admits that racist and sexist language is wrong. He explains his frustration, however, when he notes that the world is imperfect. Doing the right thing is not always easy or possible. Jane's absolutist criterion makes it impossible to resolve a conflict with other absolutist values. As a result, it is so narrowly constructed that it lacks meaningful applicability in a debate, where the purpose is to defend a means of deciding among values. An advocate should not hope to succeed by stridently asserting a single issue and refusing to justify it in the context of competing alternatives.

Some resolutions almost demand criteria that are too narrow to encourage meaningful debate. For example, the resolution, "Resolved: that violence is a justified response to political oppression," offers narrow grounds for developing criteria. Debaters frequently use the term *justified* to determine if something is legal, as in the phrase *legally justified*. A debater may be tempted to use such a criterion because the burden of proving that an act is legal is easier than proving that it is just. The standard is so narrow that it does not allow for meaningful debate.

Is the Criterion Too Vague for Meaningful Application?

By contrast to the previous line of argument, some criteria can be so broad that they lack meaningful application in a debate. Extremely vague criteria are subject to attack because they provide virtually no meaningful way to tell what is more important.

> Maury: Of course, racial tension is bad and should be avoided, but free speech should be protected. There is no way to tell which is more important.

Vague criteria, such as arguing that some value is good or bad, do not serve to provide a meaningful method for resolving conflicts. Both the affirmative and negative teams are likely to argue that their value is good and their opponent's value is bad. More meaningful approaches include determining what degree of a value is beneficial, the context in which the value is beneficial, or the overall utility of the value in its particular circumstances.

Criteria may suffer from inherent weaknesses that can make it difficult to persuade a judge that they are appropriate for the debate. Debaters should strive to discover criteria that provide a means for measuring values. They should construct the criteria to be broad enough to allow a comparison of the issues in the debate, but be narrow enough to avoid becoming too vague. If debaters can show the judge that their criteria are more appropriate and more meaningful, they will likely set the standards by which the debate will be decided.

Summary and Conclusions

Value criteria are the means used to evaluate conflicts between values. Both affirmative and negative debaters can establish criteria and should do so to decrease the judge's subjective interpretations about values. Generally, debaters have four options for arguing criteria: value hierarchy, value utility, value translation, and value context.

Value hierarchy is the prioritization of one value over other values. It is appropriate for resolutions that specify that one value is more important than another and for resolutions that argue that one value is important. Its strengths are simplicity of application and predictability. Its weaknesses include the possibility of creating absurd conclusions from too rigid an application, the tendency to ignore the probabilistic nature of value conflicts, and the susceptibility to cooption by an opponent.

Value utility is the criterion that asks whether the resolution establishes the greatest amount of good for the greatest number of people. It is appropriate for resolutions that specify how a value should be affirmed and those that indicate that one value should be the means for achieving another value. Its strengths include broadening the potential impact of the value affirmed in the resolution and providing a means for assessing the impact of a particular value. Its weaknesses are that debaters may not be able to prove the impact of one value on another, that the resulting ideal end state may not be sufficient to warrant acceptance of the value, and that competing interests may maximize the criteria.

Value translation takes two conflicting values and translates them into a single common value. It is most useful with resolutions that explain how one value should be preferred over another or ones that posit how a value should be achieved. Its strengths are that it reduces judge bias in favor of particular values and it provides a means of direct comparison between two opposing values. Its weaknesses include that the common value may not be the preeminent focus of the debate, that not all ideas are translatable into a common objective, and that your opponent can use the strategy against you.

Finally, value context is the criterion that examines values in relationship to the guidelines of particular contexts. Resolutions that specify a context or provide for exceptions in a specific context are most appropriate for this criteria. Value context is useful because it reduces the chances that debaters will overclaim the impact of an argument and it can provide the rationale for a strong, situationally persuasive defense of a claim. Lines of argument used to deny context include that values should not be based on circumstantial need, that single exceptions lead to other exceptions, and that a particular criterion may not be appropriate to the context; opponents can also coopt the context argument.

Since both teams are likely to initiate competing criteria claims, debaters must be prepared to resolve these conflicts. Generally, they should ask whether a criterion is appropriate to the resolution, to the values affirmed by the resolution, and to competing values. They should also seek to determine if the criterion provides a meaningful way to resolve value conflicts by seeing if the criterion is measurable, too narrow, or too vague. The team that defends its criterion as more appropriate to the debate and more meaningful in the evaluation process will in all likelihood have greater success in the debate.

Exercises

1. Examine a column from your newspaper's editorial page or a magazine of editorial opinion. Identify the criteria it uses to reach the conclusion. How do those criteria fit into the general lines of argument we described: hierarchy, utility, translation, or context?

2. Examine the following resolutions and identify what criterion is most appropriate for determining the probable truth of the claim. Explain why the criterion you select is most appropriate.

   Resolved: that the United States should withdraw all its combat forces from bases located outside the Western Hemisphere.

   Resolved: that American television has sacrificed quality for entertainment.

   Resolved: that affirmative action promotes deleterious hiring practices.

   Resolved: that activism in politics by religious groups harms the American political process.

   Resolved: that the U.S. Supreme Court, on balance, has granted excessive power to law enforcement agencies.

3. Using an editorial, identify the criterion used to reach the conclusion. Explain the weaknesses of that criterion for the specific value choice made in the article.

4. Take an editorial from a broadcast, newspaper, or magazine of opinion. Identify the criteria used to reach the conclusion. Establish countercriteria that would lead your audience to conclude differently.

5. Along with a partner, select a controversial claim such as those listed below and select sides, affirming and negating the claim. Each of you should present a two-minute speech establishing a criterion for determining the probable truth of the claim. In a two-minute rebuttal, attack your opponent's criterion and reestablish your own.

   Abortion is immoral.
   We should tax the rich to give to the poor.
   Flag burning is not patriotic.
   Affirmative action is justified.

4

Analyzing Justification Through Lines of Argument

Chapter Outline

Key Terms

justification
scope
magnitude
social significance
traditional importance
moral imperative
countervalues
value objections
countervalue objections
disadvantages
link
unique
impact
link turn
impact turn

George: How can you say that the school has overemphasized athletics?

Paula: We have sacrificed the integrity of the school to win a few football games. That's not a university. That's a minor league sports team.

George: I agree that the university ought to be in the business of education. But a strong athletic program isn't going to kill the school.

Paula: By making athletics a top priority, we admit students who cannot keep up in the classroom. Professors compromise their standards, and because everyone thinks of us as the "jock" school, fewer smart students apply here.

George: Well, I think the school's academic standards are fine and we have plenty of applicants for the fall class. I don't think we are hurt by athletics.

Is Paula correct that the school is compromising academics for athletics? Or is George correct that athletics poses few problems for university academics? George does not dispute the importance of education for the school, but he insists that education fares well despite the commitment to athletics.

Anyone attempting to affirm a value resolution must defend the value specified in the resolution. If both teams agree on the criteria appropriate for evaluation, the remaining task is to show, through illustrations of practical significance, how the values embodied in the resolution do or do not meet the criteria. Do the criteria match up well with the illustration, serve as useful tools in some ways but not in others, or lack any relationship whatsoever to the illustrated values? Arguments that illustrate the practical significance of a value are called **justification**.

Affirmative debaters have the responsibility to initiate justification arguments. They must convince the judge that within the context of the resolution, the value is justified. Negative debaters may choose to challenge the way that the affirmative has justified the value. The negative may also ignore the justification argument and focus on other arguments in the debate.

In this chapter we present the lines of argument that revolve around justification in value debate. Specifically, we outline the options for the lines of argument that prove that the value is justified, the options that deny that a value is justified, and the options that are useful in resolving conflicts between the two.

Lines of Argument Supporting Justification

When making a case to justify a value, affirmative debaters have a variety of argumentative strategies available. They can argue that the importance should be measured by the scope of individuals affected, the magnitude of the value to some individuals, the societal importance of the value, the traditional importance of the value, and the moral imperative of upholding the value.

Scope of the Value

Some values are easily justified by assessing the scope of their importance. The **scope** identifies the number of people to whom the value has importance. In our opening example, Paula could easily argue that overemphasizing athletics influences a large number of students.

> Paula: The number of quality applicants for the fall class has fallen in the wake of the grade-fixing scandal with the football team. The school has suffered a 10 percent drop in those seeking admission to our school.

Here, Paula argues that the lower number of quality applicants demonstrates how the overemphasis on athletics has affected the school. Paula argues that this statistical measurement justifies the conclusion that athletic programs receive too much attention. If she is correct that the quality of a student can be measured statistically in this way, then she justifies her claim. At times, specific figures for the extent of the value are not available. Faced with this situation, you can rely on approximate figures to estimate the scope of the value.

The use of a numerical standard can be very persuasive when the criterion is consistent with the justification claim. The affirmative argument implies that affirming the resolution benefits a large number of people. Affirmative debaters advocating the resolution, "Resolved: that increased restrictions on civilian possession of handguns is justified," could point to the tens of thousands of lives that handgun restrictions would save. Debaters could affirm the resolution, "Resolved: that U.S. higher education has sacrificed quality for institutional survival," by arguing that while college enrollments are up, scores on assessment tests have been declining for an ever wider portion of the student population. The number of individuals affected under both of these resolutions justifies the resolution.

Magnitude of the Value

Not all justification arguments are suited for statistical measures of their importance. A second line of argument for proving significance is the **magnitude** of the value, i.e. the degree of importance that individuals attach to the value. Even if you cannot prove that the value is important to a large number of people, you can still argue that the value is important to those people it does affect.

> Paula: Were you one of the unlucky ones that got in the classes with the Athletic Exception casualties? I was. They let in those athletes as exceptions and the teachers end up teaching to them. I've never been so bored in my life.

Paula is arguing that while the entire student body might receive a good education, a handful of students suffer from a commitment to athletics. A large number of students never have contact with a student athlete, so a large number of students may not be directly affected. However, Paula contends that compromising academic standards seriously injures a few students, leaving them with an unacceptable education.

Nothing precludes you from combining lines of argument showing both the scope and magnitude of the value being debated. Frequently, the two arguments can combine to make the most compelling justification for the resolution. Paula could identify the number of classes with Athletic Exception students and the number of students in those classes to say that an overemphasis on athletics adversely affects a large number of students.

Virtually any significant problem can be explained by the magnitude of the problem. Almost all resolutions have the potential to be justified by the magnitude of a value, but for some resolutions the magnitude of the justification is very appropriate. For example, in the resolution, "Resolved: that continued U.S. covert involvement in central America would be undesirable," it would be appropriate to discuss the potential magnitude of any U.S. covert activity. If the affirmative side elects to argue that U.S. covert activity increases the repressive tactics of right-wing dictatorships, they could describe the effects of torture on political prisoners. Or, on a larger scale, they could describe how U.S. covert actions increase the possibility of war and describe the effects of war on the environment and human life. In either case, the affirmative is hoping to appeal to the judge's desire to avoid problems because their magnitude, whether for individuals or for countries, is too great.

Social Significance

Debaters can also support a value by arguing that the value has importance to society as a whole. Unrelated to specific numbers of individuals or the effect on particular individuals, **social significance** is a line of argument holding that some values are important because they benefit society as a whole.

> Paula: The overall quality of life at the university has been terrible. Everybody feels like their degrees are worth nothing when they graduate. We know that employers are going to scoff at the school on our resumés. No one cares about achievement and it will only get worse.

Paula argues here that this is not necessarily an issue with a quantifiable effect on the student population. Nor does its direct effect on specific individuals compel sympathy. Rather, Paula feels that overemphasis on athletics demoralizes the entire university population. The effect on the university community justifies the value.

A variety of resolutions can be justified because of their social value. The resolution, "Resolved: that the trend toward increasing foreign investment in the United States is detrimental to this nation," can be justified by the effect foreign investment has on American society. Continued foreign investment, an affirmative could argue, would continue to erode the economic security of the United States. The resolution, "Resolved: that significantly stronger third-party participation in the U.S. presidential elections would benefit the political process," can be justified by the effects third-party elections would have on society as a whole. Third-party participation could improve the quality of democracy, thereby improving the political, social, and economic policies of the nation. Society provides us with the foundation for many of our beliefs about values.

Traditional Importance

The fourth line of argument proving justification is that an issue has traditional importance. **Traditional importance** argues that some conventions of nations, cultures, and communities are valuable historically. These traditions carry significant importance in value debate.

> Paula: From the school's inception it has placed educational goals as its number one priority. Never in the school's history have we been associated with any scandal that compromised academics—not until we started earning money from TV coverage of our football team! Over one hundred years of academic achievement and then, Bam! The reputation of the school is tarnished forever.

Here, Paula appeals to the tradition of the university to justify the claim that the university is overemphasizing athletics now. The longstanding importance of academic achievement in the university justifies maintaining academics as the number one priority.

Debaters should not underestimate the value of tradition as a persuasive appeal to justify affirming a value. Authorities, such as the Supreme Court, rely on the use of precedent (a respected tradition in legal jurisprudence) to serve as the basis for their legal interpretations of court cases. Likewise, debaters can use tradition as the basis for their values. Affirmative debaters using this approach could defend the resolution, "Resolved: that significant government restrictions on coverage by the U.S. media of terrorist activity are justified." They could argue that traditionally the courts have upheld First Amendment restrictions in periods threatening immediate danger. An affirmative debater could defend the resolution, "Resolved: that membership in the United Nations is no longer beneficial to the United States," by defending that United States foreign policy is traditionally isolationist. Admittedly, the United States engages in foreign policy when it has few options, but inevitably the country retreats into isolationism as soon as events allow. Traditional support for values sometimes justifies their affirmation within resolutional contexts. Traditional values can be found in topics ranging from constitutional law to foreign policy, from economic interests to social morality.

Moral Imperative

The final approach to establishing justification is the use of the moral imperative. The **moral imperative** argues that members of society have some ethical responsibilities that are fundamental to the human order. Typically, values such as justice, honesty, fairness, compassion, and honoring the family fall within this category.

> Paula: Fairness demands that athletes do not receive preferential treatment. If they cheat, they should be thrown out of school like any other student would be. If they can't compete in classes, they should flunk out of school. All students must be treated equally.

In her final argument, Paula fortifies her claim that the university has overemphasized athletics by appealing to a moral imperative. She argues that all students must be treated fairly. Other students would flunk out or be thrown out of school if they could not follow the classes without unauthorized assistance. Fairness is so fundamental in an academic setting that it should guide all students throughout their educational pursuits.

Moral imperatives can be a highly persuasive means for establishing the practical significance of a value. Society is replete with examples of individuals who have endured extreme personal sacrifice to uphold their ethical responsibilities. Whistle-blowers regularly lose their jobs or have to tolerate continued harassment in the workplace for their insistence on the proper functioning of their organizations. Society allows numerous guilty defendants to go free to preserve the principle that each individual should be presumed innocent until proven guilty beyond a reasonable doubt. Anita Hill, the woman who accused Supreme Court Justice Clarence Thomas of sexual harassment, arguably assumed great personal sacrifice for what she testified were her ethical responsibilities as a citizen. Moral imperatives maintain that the principle of upholding an ethical responsibility is a higher priority than any consequences that might result from acting in an ethical manner.

Some resolutions, due to the values they uphold, invite the moral imperative as form of justification. For example, the resolution, "Resolved: that the United States Supreme Court, on balance, has granted excessive power to law enforcement agencies," might invite arguments about the moral imperative of protecting innocent citizens from the potential of false convictions. Or, the resolution, "Resolved: that government censorship of public artistic expression in the United States is an undesirable infringement of individual rights," might invite arguments about the moral imperative of protecting free expression in a free society. In either resolution, there may exist moral justification for values which deserve consideration as transcendent moral authority which society should always support.

You should not feel limited to a single line of argument when establishing the importance of a value. Frequently, two or more of the lines of argument work in conjunction to produce the strongest possible persuasive appeal. By using a variety of these approaches, you can maximize the likelihood that you will convince the judge that a substantial justification for the value exists—an issue you must win to have the judge vote to affirm the resolution.

Lines of Argument Denying Justification

Once the affirmative establishes that a value is justified, negative debaters usually attempt to reduce the importance of the value. Like the affirmative, negative debaters have a variety of lines of argument they can use to achieve their goals. To deny the justification, they can argue that no value exists, that the value is less important than the affirmative claims, and that the value competes with other more important values.

No Value Exists

Using the first line of argument, negative debaters may choose to deny the existence of any value whatsoever. In the athletics debate, George cannot credibly deny that scores are declining or that teachers are lowering standards. He can, however, argue that the societal value that Paula claims is nonexistent. As you recall, Paula suggested that the emphasis on athletics has demoralized the campus. George denies that demoralization is a problem.

> George: Our campus is not depressed. We just won a national championship. If anything, school spirit is at an all-time high.

With this argument, George attempts to eliminate the societal justification for deemphasizing athletics. George denies Paula's claim of demoralization by arguing that winning the championship offsets any negative feelings among students and alumni. By undermining the societal foundation of the value, George completely denies one of Paula's lines of argument for affirming justification. While this does not eliminate the problems associated with the overemphasis on athletics, it does provide some perspective for viewing those affected adversely.

The argument that the affirmative can justify no value at all is rare in debate because, in most instances, affirmative debaters choose values that have some merit. Occasionally, however, the negative team will be able to argue that there is no societal or traditional value in a resolution. In defense of the resolution, "Resolved: that government censorship of public artistic expression in the United States is an undesirable infringement on individual rights," an affirmative could argue that keeping comedian George Carlin's seven dirty words off of television violates free speech, a right guaranteed by the Bill of Rights. The negative could insist that these particular words have no value. As nothing more than obscenity, they do not deserve the protections afforded to free expression.

Value Is Exaggerated

Rather than claim that the affirmative case lacks any value, negative debaters might choose to use the second line of argument, that the affirmative is over-claiming the importance of the value. This line of argument attempts to persuade the judge that the implications of the value are substantially less important than the affirmative claims.

A value can be exaggerated at any number of levels. You can claim, for example, that the affirmative team is inflating the scope of those the value affects. Here the goal is to reduce the number of individuals adversely impacted by affirming the value.

> George: Our class is just not that much worse than last year's. Sure, a few people with slightly lower GPAs and SAT scores got through the admissions net, but that's happening everywhere.

George minimizes Paula's value here in two ways. First, he suggests that the test scores and grades have only experienced a small decline. This approach directly addresses the severity of the problem. Second, he suggests that some other cause is responsible for the problem. George implies because grades and scores are dropping throughout the nation, the emphasis on athletics at this particular school cannot be entirely responsible for the problem. Both strategies reduce the quantitative scope of the justification in value debates.

If you do not think that the affirmative exaggerates the scope of the value, you might think that the affirmative exaggerates the magnitude of the value. This line of argument attempts to persuade the judge that the effects of not affirming the value on the victims are substantially less than what the affirmative claims.

> George: Professors aren't teaching down to athletes all that much. Some may simplify the language of their lectures, but the concepts are still the same.

Here, George argues that the decline of the classroom experience is not as negative as Paula claims. He admits that professors take the athletes into account, but not at the expense of class content. The result, George would argue, is that Paula exaggerates this justification for her claims.

Affirmative debaters can also overclaim the societal justification for values. The actual impact on society, either presently or in the future, may not be as horrible as the affirmative would have the judge believe.

> George: People may be taking another look at our school, but that's not going to hurt our earning potential once we get out. Our contacts with successful alumni should protect us.

With this argument George attempts to reduce the societal justification for de-emphasizing athletics. Paula suggested that the demoralization of the campus would deter businesses from being interested in the school's graduates. George denies this claim by arguing that alumni contacts will offset any decrease in prestige that the school might suffer.

The affirmative can also exaggerate claims of the traditional foundations of the value. The question of what constitutes a tradition is always open to debate. Is the tradition cited by the affirmative actually a guiding philosophy appropriate in all circumstances? Is the tradition outdated? Have circumstances changed since the reliance on tradition, making it inapplicable in current circumstances?

> George: Our school's educational mission is not limited to the best and the brightest. It has always been willing to extend help to those who had trouble meeting conventional standards for acceptance.

George indicates with this example that the school's tradition of education is much broader than Paula's interpretation. If anything, the tradition lays the foundation for accepting more athletes in the future. By doing so, the school ensures an access to education for all members of society.

The final means for exaggerating the importance of a value is to mislabel obligations as moral imperatives. Some ethical responsibilities justify personal sacrifice, but others do not. Those that fall in this latter group warrant changes in our value structures only when considered with other factors.

> George: The university does not have a responsibility to treat every student identically. If that were true, we would never admit students who required remedial training in particular subjects. It is the school's obligations to meet the needs of each student. Helping students overcome their weaknesses ought to be the goal.

Here, George demonstrates the weakness of a moral imperative that is defined too broadly. If a single exception can be found to the moral imperative, the overall claim is weakened. Taken to the extreme moral imperatives may become absurd. Be alert to sweeping claims of moral obligation. They rarely withstand careful analysis.

When debating on the negative, you can develop several approaches to each claim of justification. You can reduce the importance of the value by indicating that the scope and magnitude of the value are exaggerated. You can reduce the importance by indicating that there is minimal impact on society, that the value carries little traditional support, or that no moral imperative exists.

Competing Values Are More Important

In some instances, however, the negative may not choose to undermine the affirmative's argument that the resolution has value. Instead, the negative debater may employ the final line of argument to deny justification: that competing values are more important. Arguments that indicate that competing values are more important than the value affirmed in the resolution are referred to by many names in competitive debate circles: **countervalues, value objections, countervalue objections,** and **disadvantages.** In this text we use these terms interchangeably. Each of the terms refer to an argument that shows that the affirmative's value system leads to acceptance of inferior values or forfeiture of some greater good.

In order to establish that a competing value objection justifies the rejection of the affirmative value, the negative must prove the value competes with the affirmative value, it is more important than the value of the affirmative, and that only by affirming the value is the trade-off between the affirmative and negative value arguments created. As we go through these argumentative requirements, you will see many references to criteria-based arguments that we covered in the last chapter. This is because most negative value objections combine arguments about criteria and/or definition with their own illustrations of practical significance in order to show the shortcomings of the affirmative case. In this sense, the justification component of a debate can be made to bear wider argumentative responsibilities. Debaters need to be prepared to think about the interactions among topicality, criteria, and justification to perform effectively in this area.

JUSTIFICATION

In the final round of the 1990 Cross-Examination Debate Association National Championships, Central State University (Charles Mallard and Josh Hoe) affirmed the resolution, "Resolved: that the trend toward increasing foreign investment in the United States is detrimental to this nation." Southwest Missouri State University negated the resolution. Mr. Mallard presented the following justification to prove that the impact of economic growth caused an irreversible effect on the global environment. His original argument and Southwest Missouri State's Robert Olson's response to the argument are presented in the accompanying speeches.

Affirmative

We would argue that this growth has caused the rise in the greenhouse effect. As World Bank scientist Norman Meyers explains in the spring edition of Foreign Policy in 1989 on page 34. "Today the world's industrialized nations, such as the United States, England, West Germany, and Japan are enjoying a quality of life unsurpassed in human history. Regrettably, however, that life-style is being bought at enormous environmental costs. And one of those costs is global warming caused by the greenhouse effect."

We would argue that this risks humanity's future. Professor Murphy explains in the December 1989 edition of America magazine on page 472 that "Sooner or later, probably early in the next century but in any event in the near future of the race, the buildup of greenhouse gases on the atmosphere will have to end if humanity is to have a future."

We would note contention number one, that carbon dioxide (CO_2) necessarily does increase warming. Initially, we would argue that carbon dioxide is responsible for fifty percent of the warming that is occurring. Director Holdgate of the World Conservation Union explains in October 1989 on page 38. "The

Negative

The greenhouse effect is a fraud. Maduro in 1989. "Many highly respected U.S. scientists state that the so-called greenhouse effect is a hoax and that the behavior of the news media in perpetuating this fraud is completely irresponsible."

Next is, urban temperatures are misleading. The Associated Press in 1980. "The rise might be partly due to increasing urbanization where temperatures are recorded. City temperatures are higher . . ." (Kansas City Star, p. A5). This is a pretty funny argument. It just says that because they put the thermometers in the city, and it's warm there, it's now warming.

Next is, temperature fluctuations destroy analysis. Specter in 1990. "Temperature measurements pose another problem . . . The increase was not steady, [but] fluctuating in ways that have been difficult to understand." (p. A2.)

Last card here is that there is no consensus on [the] threshold for absolute survival. Carpenter in 1990. "Scientists have failed to build a strong empirical case that cataclysm is around the corner. Although scientists agree that the climate will change, there is no consensus about when, where, or how much." Means unless you have absolute impact, you will not vote [for the affirmative.]

(Continued)

Affirmative (Cont.)

best available estimates suggest that carbon dioxide . . . contributes fifty percent of the greenhouse effect."

Secondly, we would indicate that CO_2 growth is multiplied by status quo growth. Professor Revkin points out in the February edition of Current magazine in 1989 on page 4: "Carbon dioxide levels are twenty-five percent higher now than they were in 1860, and the atmosphere's burden of greenhouse gases is expected to keep growing."

Furthermore, we would argue thirdly that studies prove that [the] greenhouse [effect] linearly increases death as CO_2 increases. Dr. Schneider explains in The Greenhouse Century in 1989 on page 182: "An EPA-commissioned study by L. S. Kalkstein and colleagues, from the University of Delaware, suggests that total summertime heat-related mortality in fifteen U.S. cities would grow from a current estimate of nearly 1,200 deaths to almost 7,500 deaths in a CO_2 -doubled world."

Lastly, we would argue that any additional growth risks irreversible global warming, as Doctor Moore . . . warns us in 1990 in International Wildlife on page 16. "If we continue business as usual, dramatic climatic change will be inevitable— and there will be no turning back the clock." (p. 15).

Negative (Cont.)

Next is risk to human future. Of course, one response is this assumes present greenhouse situation, which I [have already argued was a fraud.] Two is, even if true, it's no big deal. Harper in 1986. "But suppose we postulate . . . greenhousing on Earth, just to see where it leads us. . . . Melting the ice caps would add roughly ten percent to the existing land-to-water ratio, all of it in the form of shallow, evaporatively efficient tidewaters." (p. 33).

Next is decreased electric use lowers CO_2 emissions. Harper in 1986. "The same heat that leads to the melting . . . also tends to increase evaporation and . . . cloud layers, which reduce the intensity of solar radiation . . ." (p. 33–34). With generally warmer temperature we need no longer use so much energy heating our homes, so the rate of CO_2 slows. Makes sense, it's warmer out, you don't heat your homes so much, means you have less energy use.

Next is, greenhouse cancels itself out. Harper in 1986. "The shallow tidewaters become prime breeding ground for . . . algae, which absorb CO_2 and release oxygen. Oceanic CO_2 . . . completes the picture and conditions stabilize, probably well short of a complete ice melt." (p. 34). This is the best card in the round. Harper in 1986 says that humans will survive. "The consequences may be rather uncomfortable [although I think they would be fairly comfortable, he says], the human race would survive." (p. 34). Without absolute survival, you don't vote [affirmative].

Linking the Value Objection

The first requirement of a countervalue objection is that it must compete with the affirmative defense of the resolution. Referred to as a **link,** this line of argument posits that affirming one value forces a choice with a competing countervalue. Negative debaters can link a value objection in two ways. First, they can claim that the affirmative justification of the value has undesirable implications. In Paula and George's argument over athletics, George might try to show how limiting athletic scholarships would deprive the university of important benefits.

> George: I think it's good for the school to provide opportunities to athletes. Professors should teach to the neediest students. If athletic exemptions bring in students who need special attention, so be it. Many athletes learn discipline through sports. Many athletes will do well in college away from weak school systems and with proper discipline. The school should serve those who need it most. Even the athlete.

Here, George links the countervalue to the affirmative justification of the value. George concedes to Paula that education is important. Noting that Paula justifies the resolution by arguing that teachers lower their level of instruction to teach to the weakest student, George seizes upon the opportunity to prove that schools compromise the value of an education if they exclude special-status students from the classroom. Special-status students need the most attention, according to George. Therefore, a vote against the resolution is a vote to maximize the values of education.

In the debate resolution, "Resolved: that increased restrictions on civilian possession of handguns in the United States would be justified," the affirmative could argue that freedom from crime is an important value that would justify many restrictions. The affirmative debater could justify the value of restrictions by arguing that increased handgun restrictions, such as waiting periods to see if a person has a criminal record, can decrease crime. The negative debater could respond by arguing that the restrictions would not be justified because they would actually increase crime. Criminals might commit more crime to obtain the expensive weapons available through the black market. Here, the negative debaters would be linking their argument to the affirmative justification. They would aim to show how increased restrictions actually compromise the value they are designed to protect. Negative debaters frequently link value objections to justification arguments while agreeing with the criteria or value affirmed in the resolution.

Another means for linking a countervalue to a justification argument is to show how the justification argument compromises another more important value.

> George: I'm in favor of admitting athletes precisely because they are different from mainstream students. It's good to have a diversity of opinion on campus, to associate with people who have something other than books and professional school on their minds. Athletes represent an important viewpoint that should be widely represented on campus.

George argues that the inclusion of student athletes exposes the average student to different perspectives on school and work. Through encounters with student athletes, nonathletes are exposed to different ways of framing their own experiences. When Paula argues that there are too many athletes on campus, George's argument gains more force. The more athletes there are, the more likely that mainstream students will experience the diverse perspectives athletes bring to the college community.

Sometimes, debaters can take this sort of value analysis to extremes. In the example of increased restrictions on handguns, for example, affirmatives are likely to justify restrictions on the grounds that they decrease crime. The affirmative assumptions hold that crimes are so bad that any decrease of crime would justify affirming the resolution. Negative debaters could respond with the argument that crime is not as bad as most people think. Property crime may even be *good* for the economy. Crime redistributes goods from the wealthy to the poor. To replace those goods, individuals buy theft insurance, which increases the investment funds of insurance companies. Wealthy consumers replace the stolen goods with new goods. By increasing spending on consumer goods, theft actually generates economic demand, which creates jobs. Crime might also be good because the fear of it drives people out of the inner city. Studies show that the inner city is more stressful because it is crowded and more polluted. Thus crime, by driving people out of the city, may actually save lives by reducing stress. These arguments are, of course, counterintuitive, but they illustrate that the affirmative justification for the value of handgun restrictions links to other more important values that will be sacrificed if the judge affirms the resolution.

Sound silly? Some of these arguments undoubtedly are, but they illustrate an important principle of thinking through the value orientations in a debate case. Avoiding a harm or obtaining a useful value may look good in isolation, but we need to consider the alternatives that necessarily come into play. This is a practice that we engage in every day. Students who go to college sacrifice earnings for many years, often living in small dormitory rooms without kitchens or private bathrooms. If we were to investigate college as a question of material lifestyle, it would almost certainly seem less attractive than most other living arrangements. Of course, we do not evaluate college in this way. We think about the sacrifices as part of a broader educational experience that is not only intrinsically valuable, but ultimately serves the material goals more effectively as well. This kind of thinking is essential to creative value-debating analysis. Do not be afraid to think through counterintuitive positions; some of them may make a great deal of sense. However, before using such arguments in a debate round, be sure you can defend them as reasonable perspectives to bring to the debate.

In sum: negative debaters can link their value objections to the affirmative's justification argument in two ways. The negative can show that the affirmative's justification actually undermines the value supported in the resolution or that it compromises some more important value. In addition to linking the value objection to the affirmative's justification argument, the negative can also find a link to the affirmative's criteria.

When establishing criteria, the affirmative argues that one value is more important than another value. Disagreeing with the affirmative assessment, negatives can link their value objections to the affirmative's rationale for choosing one value over another.

> George: I disagree. Education is not as important as the social atmosphere of the campus. Athletics helps sustain a healthy social environment. The more athletics, the better the life of the student.

George is arguing that Paula's criterion of establishing education as the top priority is incorrect. The value of education is not as important as the value of the social life of the student. Given that social life is a more important value and that athletics contributes to a wholesome campus atmosphere, the emphasis on athletics should continue.

In the resolution, "Resolved: that U.S. regulations requiring employees to be tested for controlled substances are an unwarranted invasion of privacy," the value of privacy is compared to the benefits of drug-testing. The affirmative debater could argue that privacy is more important than any state interest in drug-testing. The negative debater could link a disadvantage to this criteria. The negative could argue that the state interest should be paramount because it could save lives in critical industries, such as transportation, machinery operations, and health care, that require hand-eye coordination. In effect, the negative would be saying that the acceptance of the affirmative's criteria would result in a loss of lives. Without drug-testing, accidents would happen.

Value objections can also link to criteria when the criteria implicate values outside the resolution. In the resolution on drug-testing, an affirmative might argue that privacy is the most fundamental right human beings have. The essence of human beings, the affirmative might reason, is the ability to regulate the privacy of their own persons. The negative debater might respond that the criterion that establishes privacy as the most important right leads to undesirable consequences because it implicates other values. The negative could argue that privacy is not a fundamental right and to treat it as such leads to compromising other more fundamental rights (e.g., freedom of speech, press, and association). By establishing the right of privacy as a paramount issue, the affirmative debater risks undermining other political rights that might be of greater importance.

Uniqueness of the Value Objection

Value objections should generally have a unique link to the affirmative. A link is **unique** if the affirmative defense of the resolution alone results in the value objection. If existing interpretations of the value also link to the value objection, the argument is nonunique.

> George: Only athletics can bring the school the national reputation we would both like to see. I think the national reputation will help all students when they go out into the job market. We need athletics so that people will remember the name of the school and associate it with success.

George is arguing in this example that the reputation of the school is a very important value to the job-seeking graduates of the school. He points out how the value objection is unique by showing that only athletics is capable of bringing such a reputation to the school.

In the example of drug-testing, where the negative maintains that public safety is a more important value than privacy, the negative would have to show that drug-testing alone would ensure public safety. If the workplace had other mechanisms protecting the safety of the public (e.g., backup checks and frequent worker rotation), the unique value of continuing drug tests would no longer be present. The safety of the public would be intact regardless of whether the judge affirmed or negated the resolution.

Some controversy exists about whether a countervalue has to be unique. In some contexts, the uniqueness of a countervalue does not appear necessary. When a value hierarchy is argued as the appropriate criterion for evaluation, the need to show uniqueness is questionable. Assume momentarily that maintaining a free press is more important than guaranteeing a fair trial. It would not matter how many trials had violated the rights of the press; the hierarchy would require that any abridgement of the freedom of the press should cease.

In other contexts the negative debaters should have to prove that their countervalues are unique to the affirmative case. If utility is the criterion, for example, the negative would need to know the potential scope of populations affected by the countervalue. If people are going to experience workplace accidents whether or not drug tests exist, the negative has not established the utility of having the tests.

Some judges of value debate believe that all countervalues must be unique. Others disagree entirely, claiming that no value objections have to be unique. Given the level of confusion, debaters should be prepared to provide a rationale for the unique importance of their countervalue.

Impact of the Value Objection

A countervalue can only be persuasive if it has a significant **impact,** or relevance in the debate. George might be correct that the national athletic reputation of the school would bolster some job opportunities for graduating students. However, if only one or two graduates receive benefits because of the enhanced reputation, the argument might not justify compromising Paula's values. There are several ways debaters can show that their countervalues outweigh the justification of the affirmative.

Countervalues Can Better Meet the Affirmative Criteria

The negative could give weight to a countervalue by showing how it maximizes the affirmative's criteria. Here, the negative, George, insists that his countervalue better meets the affirmative criteria than does Paula's affirmative justification.

> George: I think that a heavy emphasis on athletics helps the educational mission of the school. It generates revenue that can be pumped back into the academic

side of the school. It produces a national reputation that will attract high-quality students who love sports. And it increases alumni contributions to the school. The university is not overemphasizing athletics at the expense of education. It is helping education by emphasizing athletics.

George is arguing that his countervalue (emphasis on athletics) is important because it maximizes the affirmative criterion (educating students) and fulfills that criterion better than the affirmative justification (deemphasizing athletics). Thus, if both Paula and George consider education to be the ultimate goal of the university, George is arguing that the best way to maximize education is to emphasize athletics.

This type of impact for the countervalue argues that negating the resolution better fulfills the affirmative's criteria than does the affirmative justification. Using this impact strategy can be very useful for debaters. The approach lets the negative agree with the affirmative criteria, bypassing a potentially large area of disagreement. Then, the only remaining question becomes whether the affirmative's value or the negative's value better meets the criteria. As you can see, this strategy focuses the debate, providing the negative an opportunity to sustain their countervalue in the most efficient fashion.

Given the importance of this strategy, we will provide several illustrations of how it would work in an actual debate. Assume that a resolution calls for an affirmative team to defend the notion that foreign investment is detrimental to the U.S. economy. The affirmative might establish the value of employment as the criterion the judge should use to evaluate the debate. Whichever team can employ more people should win the debate. The negative might argue that foreign investment increases employment opportunities by bringing more investment into the domestic economy. Without foreign investment, the negative could reason, these employment opportunities would go elsewhere. With this value objection, the negative is attempting to maximize the affirmative's criteria.

Assume that the resolution is that United States covert involvement in Central America is undesirable. An affirmative might justify the resolution by arguing that CIA failures have undermined the national security interests of the United States. They might establish national security as the criterion the judge should use to determine who wins the debate. Attempting to capitalize on this criterion, the negative might argue that covert operations have been essential to protecting the national security interests of the United States. Information gathering, paramilitary operations, and support for struggling democracies have all contributed to the overall security of the nation. With arguments such as these, the negative insists that by affirming the resolution, the judge may sacrifice the value the affirmative criterion defines as important.

Countervalues Can Better Meet Alternative Criteria

This argument insists that the affirmative criterion is incorrect and should not be used as a basis for judging the values in a debate. Rather than simply asserting some alternative value, the argument shows how countercriteria are better suited to making sense of the value issues at work in the debate round. In place of the affirmative criterion, this argument links the negative criterion to the more important value that the judge would sacrifice by affirming the resolution. This is an important step to ensure that an argument is complete.

> George: Education is important, but it is not the only purpose of a college. Colleges also have to provide a social life and support for their community. A good athletic team does that. It gives the student population an outlet for fun and social life. It gives the community an opportunity for positive interaction with the university.

Here, George is arguing that colleges have a purpose broader than only education, which athletics helps to serve. By identifying a strong social life and support for the community as an alternative criterion, he attempts to insert other important values that the judge would sacrifice by affirming the resolution. This is perhaps the most common form of lending impact to a countervalue argument.

In defense of the resolution, "Resolved: that the United States Supreme Court, on balance, has granted excessive power to law enforcement agencies," an affirmative debater is likely to argue that due process rights are of utmost importance in criminal prosecution. With this criterion established, the affirmative team could justify the resolution by showing that law enforcement officials have used their power to violate the due process rights of criminal defendants. The negative could establish a countercriterion that indicates that the fundamental purpose of the Constitution is to protect law-abiding citizens. Within this framework, any violation of due process must be considered in relation to its effect on crime control. If the negative could prove a value objection that excessive due process protections hamper crime control and illustrate the objection by showing that crime control is more important in this context, it would maximize its chance of winning the debate.

Another example is the affirmative defense of the resolution, "Resolved: that violence is a justified response to political oppression." The affirmative could establish a criterion that self-defense is an appropriate guideline for determining when violence is justified. They could try to justify their value by indicating that some groups, e.g., Palestinians and South African blacks, are justified in violent reaction because their own existence is at stake in their violent struggle. The negative could establish the countercriterion that no circumstance justifies violence because violence itself is inherently oppressive. Violence can never be an adequate response to oppression because it only perpetuates the harmful condition. By indicating that no utilitarian argument can justify violence, the negative sets up the importance of a value objection defending the effectiveness of nonviolent civil disobedience and passive resistance.

Any one of the general lines of argument for establishing criteria may also be useful in establishing countercriteria. However, the negative must prove that the countercriteria are superior to the affirmative criteria for resolving the competition between values. The negative would therefore assume the burdens of proving the weakness of the affirmative criteria, the superiority of the negative criteria, and the arguments necessary to sustain the value objection itself. If they could meet these burdens, the negative debaters would likely prevail in the debate.

At times, the countercriterion may be an implicit part of the countervalue objection rather than a stated part of the argument. If an affirmative debater establishes a criterion that indicates that the fundamental right of privacy is greater than any state interest in safety, the negative may choose to defend implicitly a criterion based on utility. The negative could argue that there is not a significant justification for concluding that drug-testing violates privacy, since few individuals undergo drug-testing. However, the few individuals who do may save the lives of many individuals whose safety may be in jeopardy. The negative is arguing that there are more individual lives at stake without drug-testing than there are individuals experiencing an invasion of privacy. The negative is implicitly arguing that the utility of the value should be an important criterion in determining which value is more important. In this way, the negative establishes an implicit countercriterion, one that it must defend if the affirmative chooses to challenge it.

In sum: there are two ways to explain why a countervalue is more important than an affirmative value. First, the value could be more important according to the affirmative criterion. Second, the value could be more important according to a countercriterion that the negative establishes. The negative can argue countercriteria either explicitly or implicitly. Regardless, the negative debater needs to establish and be able to defend the countervalue as more important than the affirmative value.

When denying the affirmative justification of the resolution, negative debaters should not feel limited to a single line of argument. Frequently, debaters can use several arguments together to help minimize and/or outweigh the affirmative justification. By using a variety of these arguments in a coordinated approach, negative debaters maximize the likelihood that they will convince the judge that there is no value to affirming the resolution or that affirming the resolution would compromise more important competing values. Winning this issue alone can persuade the judge to negate the resolution.

Lines of Argument for Comparing Competing Value Claims

When debaters attempt to resolve the issue of justification in value debates, they compare the value of affirming the resolution with the value of negating the resolution. It is important for you to realize that while each argument requires individual attention, judges will ultimately base their decisions on the weight of the arguments as a whole.

The central issues involved in the justification of competing values are similar for both affirmative and negative debaters. As a result, the remainder of this chapter will not focus on lines of argument from an affirmative or negative point of view. Instead, it will focus on a series of questions that have implications for both teams in a debate. These questions should serve as a source for the lines of argument to compare values with countervalues.

When assessing the value of affirming the resolution, three questions are central. First, *is there a significant justification for affirming the value in the resolution?* This question is primary because the affirmative debaters must be able to prove that the answer is yes to persuade a judge that they should win the debate. If the negative debater can create doubt as to whether any substantial justification for the value exists, the judge will likely see no reason for affirming the resolution.

Second, *how substantial is the justification of the value?* In most instances, the affirmative team will want to maximize the justification for the value, while the negative will want to minimize the justification of the value. After all, the resolution is more compelling if the value is important than if it is trivial. Debaters can best establish the importance of a value in relationship to the criteria in the debate. It is therefore important that the debater consider the relationship between the criteria and the competing values.

If a sufficient justification for affirming a resolution exists, the final question becomes, *are the competing values more justified than the value affirmed in the resolution?* If affirming the resolutional value trades off with other more important values, the judge would not affirm the resolution. In such an event, negative debaters might choose to admit that the affirmative value has some justification, but also try to prove that more important competing values justify negating the resolution. To assess the countervalue of the negative, both teams must analyze the justifications of these competing values. Five questions form the locus of arguments that relate to value objections.

First, *would affirming the resolution actually compete with the countervalue?* In other words, is there a link or tradeoff between the two values? Does an emphasis on athletics actually promote job opportunities for students? Or is an emphasis on athletics an irrelevant concern for most future employers?

In the drug-testing debate, the negative maintains that a link exists between drug-testing and safety in the workplace. Affirmative debaters, by contrast, could respond that there is no link between drug-testing and public safety. Affirmative debaters could argue that drug-testing is too inaccurate to deter individuals willing to take the risk of using drugs on the job. At the end of the debate, the negative debater would have to persuade the judge that a link does exist between affirming the resolution and better protecting public safety. If the debater does not, the argument would become irrelevant in the debate.

Second, *does the value in the resolution enhance the negative's countervalue?* This line of argument is known as a **link turn** because it argues that instead of one value trading off with another value, the value affirmed in the resolution actually enhances the countervalue. It "turns" the value objection to the advantage of the affirmative debater, making it an additional reason to affirm the resolution. Does an emphasis on athletics promote job opportunities for students? Or does it actually hurt the employment prospects of the students? Perhaps an emphasis on athletics compromises the academic integrity of the school and, in the process, forfeits many future employers.

In the drug-testing example, the negative argues that drug-testing is necessary to protect safety in the workplace. The affirmative might attempt to link turn the argument by showing that drug tests will actually undermine workplace safety. The affirmative might maintain that drug-testing creates a false sense of security. Drug tests are unreliable, avid drug users can circumvent them, and people will switch to other substances that are more difficult to detect. In addition to these problems, drug tests are likely to result in the reduction of other protections in the workplace. The illusion of these tests' effectiveness could remove the incentive for other safety measures. While it first appears that the affirmative debater compromises a competing value, it is sometimes possible that affirming the resolution might enhance that value.

An affirmative debater has a strong incentive to make a link-turn argument. If the debater can convince the judge that affirming the value of the resolution is instrumental to enhancing the countervalue, the judge has yet another reason to affirm the resolution. The argument transforms the issue from one that undermines the rationale for the resolution to one that provides additional support.

Third, *would the impact occur without affirming the resolution?* Previously described as the uniqueness of the value objection, this argument shows that only by affirming the resolution will a tradeoff occur with the countervalue. Is an emphasis on athletics the only way to guarantee that students have job opportunities? Or do alumni contacts and a growth economy also produce the requisite number of jobs?

In the drug-testing example, negative debaters would want to show how drug-testing uniquely results in workplace safety. If the affirmative could discover other avenues for assuring safety, e.g., strict enforcement of OSHA laws or safety education courses, the countervalue would not be unique. Without showing that the countervalue has some unique impact, the negative will be unpersuasive with the argument.

Fourth, *would the impact of the value objection, on balance, be positive or negative?* While the negative claims that to compromise a countervalue would be a bad thing, the affirmative may try to convince the judge that undermining the countervalue is really a good idea. This affirmative argument is frequently referred to as an **impact turn** because it claims that the negative impact of the value objection becomes a desirable outcome of affirming the resolution. Is there something good about college students not being able to find jobs? Will they go into the Peace Corps instead? Or perhaps they would join the military and increase the effectiveness of the all-volunteer force.

In the drug-testing debate, the countervalue is workplace safety. The impact of the argument is accidental injuries. To make an impact turn, the affirmative would need to argue that for some reason, accidents are good. The affirmative might want to say that a few small accidents are necessary for real reform in the area of workplace safety. Only when employers experience the legal liability of a few smaller accidents will they purchase critical safety gear needed in the workplace. The negative in this debate would need to show why the impact to the countervalue (accidents) is really a bad thing. Failure to do so means that the countervalue becomes another reason to affirm the resolution.

DISADVANTAGE

In the final round of the 1991 Cross-Examination Debate Association National Championships, the University of California, Los Angeles (Brian Fletcher and Jon Dean) affirmed the resolution, ''Resolved: that the United States Supreme Court has, on balance, granted excessive power to law enforcement agencies.'' Kansas State University (Rich McCullum and Dave Fillippe) negated the resolution. UCLA argued that the Supreme Court has granted excessive power to law enforcement agencies to gather and withhold information against dissidents. The negative argued that the affirmative would make it difficult for the Environmental Protection Agency [EPA] to enforce laws against pollution. Mr. McCullum offered the value objection and Mr. Dean responded for UCLA.

Negative

The third disad is increased water pollution. The A Subpoint is the EPA is a law enforcement agency according to the affirmative scope under the Freedom of Information Act. Pace Law Review in 1989: ''In Pratt, the court of appeals determined that FOIA makes no distinction on its face between agencies whose principal function is criminal law enforcement and agencies with both law enforcement and administrative functions.''

The B Subpoint is the EPA uses exemption to collect data for enforcing the Clean Water Act, Resource Conservation and Recovery Act, etc. The Pace Law Review, in 1989: ''The district court concluded that the first of the two tests was satisfied, since the plaintiff did not dispute the EPA's claim that the documents related to an ongoing investigation of alleged violations by Alyeska of the Clean Air Act and the Clean Water Act, the Resource Conservation and Recovery Act'' (Roth, p.280).

The C Subpoint is that the Clean Water Act is necessary to solve pollution. Warner argues in 1984: ''Major environmental legislation has been designed to control potential

Affirmative

They argue that the EPA needs to get information and we will have a cleaner world. First, if there is disclosure, and there is a harm from the disclosure, then there would not be disclosure. Professor Modes concludes in 1980: ''At the same time, where disclosure would serve merely to promote illicit activity or to frustrate the legitimate policies of an agency, the public availability of law enforcement manuals would not be required.''

Next response, note the consistency that I am getting with my authors. My authors are writing the impact cards at the bottom of case. Kennedy, Clark, etc. That information is good. But these are the same people who voted for these exemptions that will not cause these positions to occur. All case deals with past investigatory records.

I will now explain the six areas of exemption, that if there is danger, there simply would not be this disclosure. Mr Sobel writes in 1982: ''The 1974 amendment preserves the requirement of 'investigatory records

(Continued)

DISADVANTAGE—Continued

Negative (Cont.)

discharges to aquifers. Acts such as
the Clean Water Act, Resource
Conservation and Recovery . . . Act,
Safe Drinking Water Act, and
Comprehensive Environmental
Response Act are reducing and
controlling industrial, commercial,
and municipal facility discharges that
contribute to groundwater
contamination.''

Affirmative (Cont.)

compiled for a law enforcement
purpose' as a threshold test, and goes
on to enumerate six specific [areas]. . . .
(1) interference with enforcement
proceedings; (2) deprivation of rights
to fair trial . . .; (3) invasion of
personal privacy; (4) disclosure of the
identity of a confidential source; (5)
disclosure of investigatory techniques
and procedures; and (6) danger to life
or physical safety of law enforcement
personnel.''

My case only indicates that you
would want past records to be opened.
If you think that is going to cause a
nuclear war and all toxic waste to
cause all this, please vote negative.
[Laughter]

Finally, *will the impact of the countervalue outweigh the impact of affirming the resolution?* At some point, the debaters need to compare the value of affirming the resolution with the value of negating the resolution. How does the school's need to maintain a high academic reputation for future employers weigh against the number of employers that would affiliate with or hire students from the school because of the strong athletic program? How would the need to keep a quality educational experience weigh against the need to teach special-status students? How do all the arguments for emphasizing athletics weigh against the arguments for deemphasizing athletics?

Affirmative debaters must be prepared to argue that the value of affirming the resolution is greater than any value that the resolution compromises. In the drug-testing debate, the affirmative must be able to show that the benefits of privacy outweigh concerns about workplace safety. Negative debaters, by contrast, argue that any values that the resolution compromises are more important. The negative must show that workplace accidents would clearly justify an invasion of privacy.

Debaters attempting to resolve competing value choices must recognize that no single method of comparison is always applicable, correct, or irrefutable. Consequently, you should familiarize yourself with each strategy to have the broadest possible range of arguments available in the particular circumstance. As with all arguments in a debate, those argued more persuasively will result in a favorable judge's decision.

Summary and Conclusions

To overcome presumption against affirming the value in the resolution, affirmative debaters must present the general line of argument of justification. This line of argument maintains that a substantial rationale exists to affirm the resolution. The judge should feel compelled to agree that the resolution is justified.

In order to establish that a substantial justification exists to affirm the resolution, five lines of argument are available: affirmation of the value is justified because a large number of individuals are affected adversely; the value has important implications in a few instances; the value is important to society; the value has traditional importance; and the value is a moral imperative. Debaters may use these lines of argument in isolation or together as a comprehensive view of the justification for affirming the resolution.

To deny the justification for affirming the resolution, debaters can argue that no justification for the value exists; that the magnitude of the justification is less than the affirmative claims; and that the affirmation of the value compromises another more important value, perhaps in a more important manner. This last line of argument is usually referred to as a countervalue in debate, but it is also called a value objection or a disadvantage. To be persuasive, negative debaters must show that the countervalue links to the value affirmed in the resolution; that the impact of compromising the value is unique to affirming the resolution (in some cases); and that the impact of the value objection is greater than the impact of the affirmative justification.

To resolve competing claims about justification, debaters compare the implications of affirming the resolution with the implications of negating the resolution. To determine whether the resolution is justified, they should ask, is there a significant justification for affirming the value? If so, what is the magnitude, scope, or importance of the value? Do competing values outweigh the affirmative's justification?

To determine if competing values overwhelm the affirmative justification of the value, debaters should ask, does the value affirmed in the resolution link to a competing value choice? Would affirming the resolution enhance the competing value? Would the impact of the value objection be compromised without affirming the resolution? Will the impact of negating the value of the resolution be, on balance, positive or negative? Does the impact of the countervalue outweigh the competing value of affirming the resolution?

Debate judges will resolve controversies about the general lines of argument, justifying competing value choices by comparing the claims made, the reasoning used to explain those claims, and the evidence used to support those claims. Debaters should remember that the burden of proof for justifying the resolution rests with the affirmative, while the burden of proof for justifying a competing value rests with the negative.

Exercises

1. Obtain a copy of a popular news periodical such as *Time, Newsweek,* or *U.S. News and World Report.* Browse the issue for an article that discusses a justification for a value. How does the article establish the claims? Does it use the scope of the value, magnitude, social significance, traditional importance, or moral imperatives? Does it combine strategies? What is its persuasive effect on you?

2. Construct a value objection against a justification that supports the value of women in combat roles during military conflict. What is the link to the objection? Why is the argument unique to the value justification? What is the impact of your argument?

3. Do a five-minute speech advocating a value of your choice. What would be the benefits of affirming your value? What would be the consequences? Do the benefits outweigh the consequences? Be sure to explain why.

4. Imagine that you are defending a justification that claims that advertising degrades the quality of life for women because it stereotypes the sexes. Your opponent argues that your justification argument creates a countervalue objection. The objection indicates that advertising is essential for economic growth in society. Using the lines of argument for resolving value objections, develop at least five reasons why the value objection does not constitute a reason to reject your justification argument.

5. Pair yourself with one of your classmates. Have a debate about the justification of a value of your choice. If you are affirmative, try to persuasively argue that the value you cite is substantial and more important than any countervalues that your opponent might raise. If you are negative, attempt to assess the impact of the affirmative's justification argument and show why, on balance, the justification argument should be rejected.

5

Interaction Among Lines of Argument

Chapter Outline

Interactions that Minimize Opponent's Arguments
   Trivializing Opposing Arguments
   Making Opposing Arguments Irrelevant
   Exposing Contradictory Arguments
Interactions that Maximize Your Arguments
   Identifying Complementary Arguments
   Initiating Independent Arguments
   Repeating Critical Arguments
Summary and Conclusions

Key Terms

cross-application
trivialization
probability
time frame
brink
threshold
linear argument
specificity of impact
degree of reparability
irrelevancy
contradictory arguments
complementary arguments
independent arguments
repetition

In Chapters One through Four we introduced the general lines of argument in value debate: topicality, criteria, and justification. As we stressed in the first chapter, all arguments in debate revolve around these three arguments to determine whether the judge should affirm or negate the resolution. The affirmative must win each argument to prevail in the debate. However, you should not view each of these arguments solely in isolation. Each argument can, and should, be combined with others to establish a consistent defense of the resolution. The negative can win the debate by defeating any one of these three lines of argument. However, it is rare that the negative wins a debate by overwhelmingly defeating only one of these three lines of argument. Frequently, they must win several arguments in tandem in order to win the debate. The negative significantly enhances its chances of winning the debate if it attacks the affirmative defense of the resolution from a coordinated perspective rather than from singular attacks on the individual lines of argument.

Debate arguments can interact in six general ways: arguments may have a trivial relationship to each other; arguments may be irrelevant to each other; arguments may contradict each other; arguments may complement each other; arguments may independently support the overall position; and arguments may be repetitious of each other. The first three forms of interaction (trivial, unrelated, and contradictory) tend to minimize your opponent's arguments. The latter three forms of interaction (complementary, independent, and repetitious) tend to reinforce your own position.

Understanding how arguments interact is critical to understanding how to approach a debate strategically. If you merely deny every argument your opponent offers, you will make several mistakes in the debate. You will waste your time answering arguments unnecessarily, fall into strategic ploys of your opponent, and undermine your own arguments. Debaters who are acutely aware of argumentative interaction may engage in strategically successful debate. When debaters use an answer to one position as an answer to another position, they engage in the **cross-application** of arguments. Cross-application can make speeches more efficient, argument selection more effective, and debates more interesting.

We devote the remainder of this chapter to identifying how the general lines of argument may interact so that you can become aware of the potential interaction that may occur in any given debate. After we identify the relationships, we discuss the strategic implications for constructing and resolving arguments. The first section of the chapter discusses arguments that minimize your opponent's position; the second section discusses arguments that maximize your own position. A debater will want to use both in tandem for maximum effectiveness.

Interactions that Minimize Opponent's Arguments

For many judges, debate is the process of cost-benefit analysis. They seek to determine the costs and benefits of affirming the resolution. In order to place your own arguments in the most favorable light, you must be able to reduce the impact of arguments that your opponent presents. By taking this step, you improve the chances that the judge will deem your own arguments to be more substantial. To minimize your opponent's arguments, you can argue that they are trivial, unrelated, or contradict other arguments in the debate.

Trivializing Opposing Arguments

In a debate where the topic is relatively balanced, where there is a fair division of ground, and where the debaters have relatively similar levels of argumentation and presentation skills, the debate may hinge on your ability to trivialize the importance of your opponent's arguments while maximizing the importance of your own arguments. **Trivialization** is the process of reducing the impact of a specific argument in the context of an entire debate. Close debates usually hinge on the ability of the debater to convince the judge to resolve comparable arguments favorably. The ability to distinguish trivial from substantial relationships is a critical-thinking skill necessary for thoughtful argumentation.

Most of us place a high value on life. If you could save one life without negative consequence, you would probably save that one life. If, however, saving one life required you to forfeit the freedom of 200 million people, you might well decide not to save that one life. The scope of freedom lost for 200 million people is arguably so much greater than the scope of one life lost that most of us would sacrifice that life to preserve freedom for so many, even if we think that life is more important than freedom. A debater would attempt to trivialize the magnitude of the loss of life in comparison to the scope of the lost freedom.

Assessing the impact of two competing positions is one of the most difficult prospects in a debate. In many debates both sides will be winning some arguments that the judge must compare to the impact of the opposition's arguments. The six most frequently used arguments for resolving the impact of competing claims are probability, magnitude and scope, time frame, linearity and threshold, specificity of impact, and degree of reparability. These arguments are usually essential for a judge to evaluate which arguments have a trivial or substantial relationship on who should win the debate.

Probability

When attempting to resolve impact conflicts, a primary question you should ask is, what is the probability of either impact occurring? The **probability** is the likelihood that one thing will lead to another. An impact to an argument can be extremely significant, but the probability of that impact occurring may be so sufficiently low that the risk may be worth taking. Human beings take chances with their lives regularly because they enjoy activities that provide thrills. Humans skydive, race stock cars, and go hang gliding. Each of these activities endangers lives while providing a thrill. People can minimize the probability of danger with safety equipment, training, intelligence, and physical prowess. They minimize the probability of losing their lives for the certain thrill of engaging in the activity. Arguments that are more probable are frequently more persuasive than arguments that have more impact but are highly improbable.

Magnitude and Scope

A second question you should ask is, how substantial is the impact? More consequential arguments are frequently more persuasive arguments. Physical activity, for example amateur sports, can result in injury to many people who participate. However, most amateur sports, such as basketball, softball, hiking, and jogging, result in minor injuries that most participants are willing to risk because their impact is so small. To achieve the positive outcomes of participation, ranging from fun to overall physical conditioning, most of us are willing to risk a sprained ankle or shoulder. If you can maximize the impact of your own arguments while minimizing the impact of your opponent's arguments, you will be more persuasive.

Time Frame

A third question you should ask is, in what time frame is the impact likely to occur? The **time frame** of an argument involves when the outcome of an argument is likely to occur. Frequently, people make important decisions on the basis of immediacy rather than by impact or probability. Many individuals smoke cigarettes, drink alcohol excessively, or eat fatty foods because such consumption provides immediate gratification. The probability that these activities may shorten their lives by several years does not deter the behavior. The risks are just too far into the future. The time frame argument can be persuasive if we determine that the immediate benefits are worth pursuing.

Frequently a tension exists between the probability of impacts, the magnitude and scope of impacts, and the time frame to the occurrence of impacts. It is often difficult to discern which of these three arguments is most important. Many who play amateur sports are willing to risk small injuries for the enjoyment of the sport. However, many of those individuals will not risk skydiving or hang gliding because the impact of that sport, perhaps less likely than a twisted ankle in other sports, is too risky for those willing to risk small injuries. Many individuals willing to smoke and drink are not willing to skydive or play basketball. Different individuals have different perspectives, which lead some to focus on probability, others on immediacy, and still others on the ultimate impact.

The debate resolution, "Resolved: that the United States Supreme Court, on balance, has granted excessive power to law enforcement agencies," contains the potential for many conflicting scenarios among probability, impact, and time frame. An affirmative debater, Niko, might defend the resolution by arguing that the Court has permitted the use of evidence that the police obtain illegally. Prosecutors can use evidence obtained without a warrant or without probable cause against defendants if the police do not knowingly violate the defendants' Fourth Amendment rights. Niko could argue that the police will use this newly granted authority to perform random searches on citizens without justification. The probability that individuals will suffer harassment and a loss of privacy increases as the police increase the number of warrantless searches. Protecting innocent civilians is, therefore, an important value threatened by the Supreme Court's decisions.

Niko's opponent, Eve, could raise a countervalue objection: that warrantless searches are necessary to win the war on drugs. Law enforcement needs the authority to prosecute drug offenders and traffickers, even if police obtain the evidence without a warrant. If the government appears soft on drugs at this time, it could destroy the public's willingness to wage a war on drugs. Drug use is destroying the moral fabric of the nation and causing deaths from crime necessary to support expensive drug habits. At this time, Eve reasons, it may be worth sacrificing some rights to prevent the ravages of drugs.

Both debaters must compare the probability of their individual impacts with the probability of their opponent's impact. If, at the end of the debate, the judge decides that one impact is more probable but that the other impact is likely to occur sooner, how does the judge decide which is more compelling? Should the judge vote to avoid the more certain harm or to avoid the near-term harm? Resolving these conflicts is the debater's responsibility. You need to provide arguments to guide the evaluation of the debate toward your position.

Despite the difficulty in doing so, debaters must frequently convince a judge that one of these issues should be the deciding factor in the evaluation of a debate. Is a short-term time frame more important than a certain impact? Is the magnitude of an impact more important than a certain impact? To illustrate how debaters make these types of comparisons, let's examine a few options for the debate between Niko and Eve.

Time Frame Outweighs Probability. Eve wants her argument that warrantless searches are necessary in the drug war to outweigh Niko's claim that innocent individuals will have their constitutional rights abridged. Eve has four options: she can argue that time frame concerns are more important than probabilistic judgments; she can attempt to reduce the probability of her opponent's scenario; she can minimize the impact of her opponent's scenario; or she can argue that her approach does more to eliminate problems than Niko's.

Eve could argue directly that the time frame of her argument is more important than a probable outcome because we must avoid the most immediate problem. If we can hold the line against drugs in the short term, we can restore constitutional privileges later. Through this argument, Eve suggests that while constitutional freedoms are important, they can survive whatever minor problems they may encounter while the nation prosecutes the drug war.

Besides demonstrating that the time frame is more important, Eve might want to undermine the probability of Niko's impact. After all, experience gives us good reason to believe that the police do not typically harass innocent citizens. The police only search suspected criminals without a warrant. If the police find no evidence of a crime, then they cannot bother innocent civilians. The police are well trained in the rules of evidence, so that they realize they must obey constitutional procedures whenever possible. If several factors combine to minimize the probability of a given outcome, the opposing argument loses much of its force. Niko's initial claim that the police will violate the constitutional freedoms of many innocent citizens is not as probable as he claims.

Third, Eve might want to concede that Niko's scenario is certain, but point out how little of a problem it really poses. The probability of a scenario is meaningless if there is no impact to the scenario. The police may search individuals more frequently. However, innocent people can obtain redress in the courts if the police are deliberately harassing them. Only evidence obtained as part of a good faith effort to enforce the law is permissible in court; improperly gathered evidence will be thrown out during a trial.

Finally, Eve could argue that whatever importance attaches to the scenario, her approach is the only way to solve the problem. If she can show that the police become abusive only when they feel they are losing the war against crime, she may well be able to convince the judge that her approach is actually safer in constitutional terms. This last method is a means of comparing ultimate results rather than minimizing Niko's claim per se. But the purpose is to minimize the effectiveness of Niko's scenario by showing that his problem, if true, deals with a smaller portion of the relevant values.

With each of these arguments, Eve bolsters her claim that the time frame of her drug war scenario should be a more important factor than the probability level of Niko's claim that innocent people will lose their rights. To show that the probability outweighs the time frame, Niko should simply ask himself the same questions in reverse. Why should probability be the most important issue? Is the time frame on Eve's scenario really short? And is there any impact to Eve's scenario if it does occur?

Impact Outweighs Time Frame. Here, Niko wants the impact of his constitutional rights argument to outweigh the short-term time frame in Eve's drug war argument. Niko has two options. He can argue that the impact of his argument outweighs the impact of Eve's argument even if her argument is more immediate. Niko can also argue that the impact of Eve's argument is not probable in the short term.

As before, Niko's first option is to claim directly that the impact of an argument outweighs the time frame. If Niko can prove that the police will violate the constitutional rights of some individuals, he can bolster the argument that any loss of constitutional rights outweighs the social good of prosecuting the drug war. The country may reduce the harm from drugs in the short term, but pays the cost of constitutional liberty in the long term. Here he would refute Eve's claims that constitutional freedoms, once lost, are easily recovered.

Niko's second approach could be to argue that positive effects from the war on drugs are not probable. If the consequence is unlikely, it does not matter when it might occur. Niko could point out that the drug war only causes the price of drugs to climb, resulting in a spiral of increasing crime and, ultimately, in more drug-related death and violence. It does not decrease the supply of drugs. If the desirable consequence is improbable, time frame is not relevant.

With these two arguments, Niko can bolster his claim that the impact of an argument should outweigh the time frame of a less-important, less-probable event. In response, Eve would examine why time frame outweighs impact arguments, whether Niko's impact really is as important as he says it is, and the actual probability of Niko's claim that constitutional liberties will be lost.

In debate, you have the opportunity to persuade the judge whether probability, time frame, or impact should guide the decision. These general lines of argument need to be developed into specific lines of argument on which any given debate pivots. Develop some specific lines of argument for the types of impacts you are comparing in order to persuade the judge that you have the stronger position on probability, time frame, and impact of competing value programs. Your ultimate goal is to maximize the strengths of your argument while trivializing the strengths of your opponent's argument.

Threshold and Linearity

A fourth method of comparing impacts is the use of threshold and linearity. The effect of an event occurs in different ways. Sometimes a chain of events is put into place leading to a point at which the event becomes inevitable. The point at which an impact becomes inevitable is called the **threshold** or **brink** of the argument. For example, debaters sometimes argue that international relations may deteriorate to the point where war becomes inevitable. That *point of no return* is a classic example of a threshold or brink. This phraseology is not unique to debate. When there are substantial international tensions, the media use the very phrases, *threshold of war* and *brink of war*, to describe these situations. If Eve could argue that we are on the brink of winning the war on drugs now, she could enhance the persuasiveness of her claim that now is a bad time to retreat from a firm commitment to fight against drugs. She could argue that we need this time to succeed in the war on drugs before we begin to protect those few innocent victims of the drug war.

Other effects, by contrast, unfold gradually as the cause of the problem increases. Rather than establish a threshold point where an impact becomes inevitable, a **linear argument** establishes that for every incremental increase in cause, there is an inevitable incremental increase in effect. Some experts say that there is a linear relationship between the consumption of cigarettes and the incidence of lung cancer. The more people smoke, the more cases of lung cancer will occur. This is a classic example of a linear relationship. In our debate, Niko might argue that there is a linear relationship between warrantless searches and convictions of innocent people. Niko argues that the number of searches increases the amount of innocent suffering in a linear fashion. The more warrantless searches there are, the more wrongful convictions there are.

Arguments based on threshold relationships can be persuasive because the arguments sound very urgent. Debaters can discuss the closeness of the threshold, emphasize how much closer added causes can push us to the threshold, and note the irreversibility of crossing the threshold. Arguments based on linear relationships can be persuasive because the debater can emphasize that any increment in cause is certain to create an equal increment in harmful effect. Such arguments can remind a judge that even small actions will have some consequence.

When debaters compare one threshold argument to another threshold argument, judges can resolve the debate by approximating which side is more likely to cross the threshold. When they compare one linear argument to another linear argument, judges can resolve the debate by approximating which side is more likely to generate a greater cause and effect. However, when comparing a threshold relationship with a linear relationship, it is sometimes difficult to develop a clear comparison. The circumstances that would trigger the impact of both arguments are so dissimilar that it may be difficult to develop a clear rationale for choosing one value over another.

Exploiting some general weaknesses of both threshold and linearity arguments will enable debaters to trivialize the impact of their opponent's position. Generally, if an impact is on the threshold of occurring, there are many potential causes that will result in that impact. Niko could agree with Eve that we are on the threshold of succeeding in the war on drugs. However, many factors are making the war on drugs a potential success, such as education for children, campaigns by sports groups, and increased enforcement of drug laws. Niko could argue that those factors that have brought us to the brink of winning the drug war are far more likely to lead to a successful conclusion of the drug war than indiscriminate searches by the police. The arguments that prove that we are on the brink also prove that crossing the threshold does not uniquely require negating the resolution. (See Chapter Four on justification for an exploration of uniqueness arguments.)

Generally, if there is a linear relationship between cause and effect, there is some doubt as to how much unique increase in a given effect occurs from any one cause. Eve could agree that police searches will violate some constitutional rights. But the potential for innocent people suffering is so unlikely that the effect is nearly impossible to define. Innocent people won't have evidence that can be used against them. Many civilians will never have contact with the police. Few constitutional rights will actually be lost. The linear relationship has such minimal effect that it is not significant enough to justify the resolution. You should familiarize yourself with the interaction between linear and threshold issues so that you can become an effective debater. Sometimes linearity and threshold questions may be difficult to resolve, but debaters who can resolve these conflicts will improve their chances of winning the debate. Good debaters should be able to maximize the strength of their own argument while trivializing their opponent's claim.

Specificity of Impact

Another option for trivializing an opponent's arguments occurs in relationships between generalized and specific impacts. The **specificity of impact** is determined by the degree of detail provided for the argumentative scenario. At times, your opponents may impact an argument with a very specific scenario to explain the implication of their argument. At other times, your opponents may impact an argument with a very general implication that does not specify a scenario in which the impact will occur.

We use the terms *general* and *specific* here rather differently from the way we used them in the core text. There, we used the terms in a technical sense to refer to broader and narrower lines of arguments. Here, general impacts are inexplicit categories of effect, while specific impacts are precise statements of the values at issue. For example, if we were to tell you that failure to finish college could "damage your future," we could support our argument with facts and figures showing lower average earning potentials and other socioeconomic indicators proving our point. Nevertheless, the impact would be quite general. "The future" is an awfully big area; it could mean practically anything. If, on the other hand, we were to warn you against the career satisfactions you might forsake by passing up a pre-med curriculum, we could be quite specific about the impact on that one hypothetical career path.

Both general and specific approaches to providing impact have advantages and disadvantages. A general approach covers a broad range of possible cases, but cannot offer very detailed information in any one of them. A specific approach can provide very precise information, but can easily be co-opted and might fail entirely to address the concerns of the judge or the arguments of an opponent.

In our debate, Niko might argue that his position is stronger because he can identify a specific impact on individuals. Certain individuals will be detained unjustifiably and searched without a warrant and without probable cause. The harassment suffered by these individuals is precise and severe. The weakness of this specific impact is that Eve could argue that society would propose targeted programs to solve the particular problem. Police training could improve. The police could be alerted to the need to respect constitutional liberties. Because the impact is specific, debaters can resolve it in specific ways. By contrast, Eve's position could be stronger because the effects of the drug war can be general or specific. Eve could argue that the drug war is necessary to solve specific problems such as the crime associated with drugs and the spread of illnesses such as AIDS and hepatitis. Or Eve could argue a more generalized impact to losing the war on drugs, such as decay of the social fabric and loss of moral character. If Eve elects to argue a more generalized scenario, then Niko could argue that the specific scenario of lost constitutional liberty is more certain and predictable.

You should be constantly alert to arguments that may distinguish between the circumstances that might lead to a specific impact and those circumstances that might lead to a more generalized impact. You should be able to use the differences between specific and generalized impacts to trivialize your opponent's impact while magnifying your own impact.

Degree of Reparability

A final line of argument for comparing the impact of two arguments is the **degree of reparability.** This standard considers whether or not society can recover from the effects. Some harms are difficult to endure, but are nonetheless tolerable if recovery is possible. It would certainly be better for most of us if the economy never again suffered from a recession. However, if we had to endure another recession we would probably survive it. Other impacts are not reparable. Certainly the damage suffered from a nuclear war could be difficult to overcome. Many environmentalists are concerned that a vast number of environmental problems are already beyond recovery: depletion of the ozone layer, global warming, and so on.

In our debate, we see opportunities for both sides to emphasize the irreparable nature of the harms. Niko could argue that the harassment suffered by innocent individuals can never be restored. Anyone subjected to the abuses of civil rights suffers irreparable trauma. Eve, on the other hand, could be arguing that if the drug war continues unabated, society could suffer irreparable damage to its moral fabric. Once the moral fabric decays, the prospects for reclaiming the values society has lost are remote.

As a debater you must develop the skills necessary to distinguish trivial from substantial relationships when advocating competing values. In this section, we have outlined some of the possible arguments that can be used to exploit this interaction. These possibilities are not limited to the arguments discussed here, but they provide a starting point for comparing competing impacts in a debate and other forums.

Making Opposing Arguments Irrelevant

Debaters frequently have to deal with arguments that are simply irrelevant. An **irrelevancy** is an argument that has no necessary bearing on the issue at hand. We could argue, for example, over the best way to get from New York to Philadelphia. After a while, you might tire of the argument and point out that it is irrelevant, because you plan to travel between New York and Boston. As a debater, you may find that some of your opponents' arguments may not be relevant to the final outcome of the debate. You may also find that some of your opponents' arguments render yet other arguments irrelevant. Debaters should be alert to irrelevancies. A judge who is persuaded that an opposing argument is irrelevant is unlikely to weigh that argument against you when evaluating a debate round.

First, topicality arguments may make some arguments irrelevant. At times, the concession of a topicality argument can render countervalue objections irrelevant. We can find one such example in our debate on the resolution that the Supreme Court has granted excessive power to law enforcement. Assume that Niko attempted to justify the resolution in two ways. First, Niko might have argued that warrantless searches violate constitutional liberties. Second, Niko might have argued that searches of high school students' lockers violate constitutional liberties. Eve could argue that the second justification is not a topical justification for the resolution. That is to say, the use of the high school example does not address the issues or values contained in the resolution. High school authorities are not law enforcement authorities; therefore, this particular justification is not topical. Eve could also offer a countervalue objection based on school discipline. Eve could argue that school discipline is justified where a school is responsible for minors. Locker searches are a reasonable practice to sustain discipline.

If Eve answered the second justification with both arguments, she would make a terrible mistake. Why? Because Niko could take advantage of the interrelationship between topicality and the countervalue objection to dismiss Eve's arguments. Niko could simply grant Eve's topicality argument that school authorities are not law enforcement. Niko could dismiss Eve's countervalue because it links to a nontopical justification. The resolution has no effect on school discipline if law enforcement personnel do not conduct school searches. Eve's value objection is irrelevant and Niko could focus his attention on the first justification of constitutional liberties. Eve's topicality argument makes her value objection irrelevant.

Second, causality and link arguments may make some arguments irrelevant. (See Chapter Six of the core text for causality arguments and Chapter Four of this text for link arguments.) In Chapter Four we noted that countervalue objections link to either the affirmative's criteria or justification arguments. An affirmative with multiple justifications for affirming the resolution can concede those that link to countervalue objections and focus instead on other justifications.

Assume again that Niko advanced two independent justifications proving that the Court has granted excessive power to law enforcement. His first justification is that innocent individuals will be convicted because of the more lenient warrant requirement. His second justification is that police become corrupted if they do not have to obey strict rules of evidence. Eve would make a mistake if she denied the first justification argument, and then linked a value objection to it; Niko could concede that Eve is correct that innocents will not be convicted. As a result, the value objection becomes irrelevant, and the issue of police corruption justifies affirming the resolution.

Affirmative debaters may also make the mistake of rendering arguments irrelevant by denying links to value objections. In our debate, let's assume that Eve admits that some innocents might have to suffer and some corruption might occur. At the same time, however, she insists that we must prosecute the war on drugs. Niko could respond to the drug war value objection in two ways. He could maintain that the war on drugs does not affect drug consumption. The war on drugs does not affect drug supplies because dealers can too easily smuggle drugs into the country and too easily produce drugs in the country. As a second response to the value objection, Niko could argue that the war is counterproductive. When the war succeeds, the cost of drugs rises. Addicts need more money for drugs so they commit more crimes. Choosing not to answer Niko's argument that the drug war actually increases drug problems, Eve could elect to concede Niko's first argument that the war on drugs has no effect on supplies. If the war on drugs has no effect on supplies, then the impact of the value objection (increased crime) is negligible. Paying attention to interrelationships can allow you to avoid answering "turned" value objections. Eve can now focus her attention on other arguments that can win her the debate.

Third, uniqueness arguments may interact to make some arguments irrelevant. Affirmative debaters will argue that affirming the resolution does not uniquely compromise another value. Against Eve's value objection about the war on drugs, Niko makes two answers. First, he argues that the effectiveness of the war on drugs is not unique to law enforcement. Niko argues that public education and drug treatment are responsible for any success in the drug war. Second, Niko argues that the war on drugs is bad. Decreasing the sale of drugs would place several Central American economies in danger of collapsing. A successful war on drugs would be worse than no war on drugs.

Niko has made the mistake of rendering his second argument irrelevant. Niko has argued that law enforcement has no unique effect on the drug trade because drug education and treatment are responsible for the decline in drug sales. Eve could concede Niko's uniqueness argument and also dismiss his second argument, that a successful prosecution of the drug war is bad economics. If law enforcement has no effect on the drug trade, it has no effect on the economy of the drug trade. Central American economies will collapse with or without increased enforcement. Eve can then devote her time to other arguments to win the debate.

There are other ways in which arguments may interact to render some arguments in the debate irrelevant. You should be alert to this possibility when planning and constructing your answers to potential arguments. You may find it beneficial to identify the arguments that render other arguments irrelevant so that you can devote your time to arguments that improve your chances of winning the debate.

Exposing Contradictory Arguments

At times, debaters can make the serious error of contradicting their own arguments. **Contradictory arguments** are those that disprove assumptions or claims made previously by the same side in a debate. You should be careful to avoid contradicting your own arguments. You should also be alert for contradiction in your opponent's arguments. Contradictions can occur in the supporting claims for individual arguments and across very distinct arguments. In this section we discuss some contradictions that frequently occur across arguments.

In some debates, negative debaters will contradict their own arguments. A likely combination of potentially contradictory arguments exists between negative countervalues and attacks against the affirmative criteria. If the negative argues that the affirmative criteria are invalid and then impacts its own countervalue according to the same criteria, the negative undermines the impact of its value objections. For example, Eve denies Niko's criterion that constitutional rights are important values in comparison to the benefits of the war. She impacts the value objection by arguing that failure to appear tough on drugs will lead to a conservative backlash, resulting in a greater loss of constitutional rights. The interaction between Eve's criteria arguments and value objection is contradictory. A judge could ignore one or both of her arguments.

Affirmative debaters may also contradict their own arguments. In Chapter Four of this text we discussed two types of turnaround arguments. One turns the link to the value objection by arguing that affirming the resolution supports rather than compromises the value. The second turnaround turns the impact to a value objection by conceding that the affirmative compromises the value but maintaining that to do so is desirable. To make both types of turnaround arguments to the same value objection is the most dangerous form of contradiction a debater can make. This contradiction is usually called a *double-turn* because the affirmative claims two distinct kinds of turnarounds: link turns and impact turns. For example, if Eve raises the value objection that the credibility of the judicial system decreases if it does not appear tough on criminals, Niko could take two approaches. He could argue that increasing privacy rights would actually increase respect for the judicial system because the public supports the system when it respects constitutional liberties (link turn). Or Niko could argue that respect for the courts is not good because it increases judicial power and disrupts the separation of powers between the Congress, the president, and the Court. Too much power, Niko could argue, would be bad for the judiciary (impact turn). If Niko makes both turnaround arguments, link turn and impact turn, he contradicts himself and can easily lose the debate. If Eve concedes both arguments, Niko increases respect for the Court, which results in making the judiciary too powerful.

There are many ways debaters can contradict themselves. We have outlined a few of the most common contradictions and explained how debaters can capitalize on them. You should always be alert to the possibility of contradiction. When developing and selecting arguments to use in a debate, be sure that they are consistent. Watch for these kinds of mistakes by your opponent. Even the best and most experienced debaters make these kinds of errors. Taking advantage of these kinds of mistakes can make you a very successful debater.

Interactions that Maximize Your Arguments

Having minimized your opponents' claims, the next step is to ensure that you are maximizing your own. By capitalizing completely on your winning arguments, you improve the judge's assessment of the competing values. Using the strategies of complementary arguments, relying on independent claims, and repeating critical points can improve your chances of winning the debate.

Identifying Complementary Arguments

At times, your opponent can make arguments that prove your arguments are true. These claims called **complementary arguments** support the reasoning of other claims in the debate. We cite several examples here, but you may discover other lines of argument that complement your arguments in any given debate.

Negative debaters may use affirmative justifications to prove the links to their own value objections (see Chapter Four of this text for a complete discussion of value objections). In the law enforcement and privacy debate, Niko might argue that a large number of individuals have had their privacy violated for the purpose of law enforcement. Eve might be willing to concede that many rights have been violated. However, Eve might argue that the rights violations are justified because they result in increased numbers of arrests and convictions. There is always danger in conceding the impact to an opponent's argument for the purpose of creating a link to another argument, but it can be a successful strategy if done carefully.

Second, the negative debaters can use the affirmative criteria to impact their own value objection. Eve could use her conservative backlash argument to prove that Niko violates his own criteria. If the court appears soft on crime, the population will demand more strict crime control measures than currently exist. In the wake of anticrime populism, many more constitutional liberties will be lost than are being lost now. In this way, Eve uses Niko's criteria to complement her own value objection. If constitutional liberties are so important, then we should not risk arousing the anti-civil liberties movement.

The affirmative also has ways to use negative arguments to support its own defense of the resolution. Affirmatives can frequently turn value objectives into arguments which support the resolution (see Chapter Four of this text for a discussion of impact and link turns). When Eve argues that we need to have strict law enforcement to win the drug war, Niko could turn the argument and claim it as an advantage. If the justice system respects constitutional freedoms and administers the law fairly, then citizens will cooperate with the courts. As a result of public respect, the drug war will be more likely to succeed. Niko uses Eve's argument—that the drug war needs to be successful—to further his own case.

Many ways exist for your opponent's arguments to actually prove that your own arguments are true. You must be alert to the possibility and carefully explain how these arguments prove your argument. Be careful not to concede the ultimate impact of the argument to your opponent. With this awareness and attention to explanation, you should be able to take advantage of these forms of argument.

Initiating Independent Arguments

Independent arguments are claims that rely on no other claims in the debate to serve as a reason to affirm or negate the resolution. In our example, Niko could justify the resolution in more than one way. He could argue that both constitutional rights and improved public safety justify the resolution. In this way, he offers two independent justifications of the resolution. If either argument proves the resolution is true, then Niko could win the debate by defending only one of the two arguments.

Negative debaters may also offer independent lines of argument. Frequently, a negative debater might offer two value objections that are quite independent of each other in how they link to the affirmative or in how they impact against the affirmative. For example, Eve might argue two independent value objections. First, she could argue that the drug war is important. Constitutional liberties may need to be sacrificed on the altar of criminal justice to ensure successful law enforcement. Second, Eve might argue that a conservative backlash could endanger many more constitutional liberties. These two arguments do not share a link or an impact. Each argument is an independent value objection. If one of the arguments is defeated, it is still possible that the other value objection will win the debate.

Other varieties of independent arguments are available to support and deny resolutions. The affirmative can argue independent criteria, independent definitions to make its case topical, and independent reasons to reject countervalues. The negative can argue that there are independent countercriteria, independent arguments to defeat the affirmative justification, and independent links and impacts to its countervalues.

The advantage of independent arguments is that it is easier for you to concede some arguments without forfeiting the entire debate. You must be sure of the independence of your claims, however, or previously discussed interrelationships may emerge to undermine your chances of winning the debate.

Repeating Critical Arguments

Communication studies show that **repetition,** or the rephrasing of arguments, can be a very persuasive strategy for the public speaker. Repetition can also be effective in debates. Repetition is a particularly important means for emphasizing when an opponent has conceded an important argument to remind the judge of the concession. It can also be helpful to reiterate arguments you believe a judge might not understand. Finally, it is sometimes useful to repeat evidence, or the particular phrasing of a quotation, to remind the judge of the impact of a particular evidenced argument on other arguments in the debate.

However, debaters should be aware of two important problems with repetition. First, debaters usually compete in timed speeches, and it may be an inefficient use of time to repeat arguments that are clear to everyone in the debate. You rarely have time for repetition. Second, be aware that repeating an argument several times in the debate provides an opponent several opportunities to answer the argument. Thus, if you repeat too much, you provide your opponent with a tactical advantage. Debaters should reserve the use of repetition for those circumstances where a memorable quotation or particular phrase aids the persuasive process. Excessive repetition merely wastes your valuable speaking time and provides tactical opportunities for your opponent.

Summary and Conclusions

Debaters need to be acutely aware of the interaction between arguments before and during debates. Being aware before the debate allows you to construct the most defensible and consistent positions. Being alert for interactions during debates allows you to take advantage of mistakes by opponents. It is not easy to process all of the arguments in a debate without making an error. The best debaters in the nation frequently contradict or fail to notice their opponent's contradictions. Intelligent debaters can take advantage of these mistakes if they are alert for interactions among arguments.

We described six types of interactions among arguments. The first three tend to minimize the impact of your opponent's arguments; these render some arguments trivial, some irrelevant, and some contradictory. The next three ways arguments interact maximize your own position: identifying complementary arguments, relying on independent claims, and repeating critical arguments.

By understanding these interactions, you should be able to approach debates with a sense of strategy. You should develop consistent, coherent positions for debating your side of the resolution. The more coordinated your own position is, the greater the chances are that you will persuade the judge to support your position.

Exercises

1. Laboratory tests reveal that animals exposed to saccharin have higher cancer rates than those that do not. Nevertheless, people who rely on sugar substitutes reduce their intake of sugar, decreasing the chances of suffering heart attacks due to obesity. Do a cost-benefit assessment of choosing to rely on saccharin. Should you use the sugar substitute? Use probability, time frame, and impact assessments to help reach your final conclusion.

2. Some commentators argue that boxing is detrimental because it can lead to severe head injuries for the participants. Imagine that you are negating the commentator's contention. Can you trivialize the commentator's argument? Use probability, time frame, and impact arguments to help you reduce the relevance of the argument.

3. Examine the editorial page of your local newspaper. Find examples of problems that commentators say we are on the brink or threshold of experiencing. Afterwards, look for examples of problems that have linear risks. Is one more persuasive to you? Why?

4. Suppose you are advocating the resolution, "Resolved: that increased restrictions on civilian possession of handguns in the United States would be justified." Your opponent has two responses: 1) the resolution is not needed because localities are already moving to adopt waiting periods for the purchase of guns; and 2) increased restrictions would violate the citizenry's right to bear arms. Can you trivialize the opponent's arguments? Can you make them irrelevant? Do they contradict? Without researching the arguments, how can you minimize the impact of your opponent's arguments?

5. Suppose you are defending a resolution, "Resolved: that individual rights of privacy are more important than any other constitutional right." Your opponent defends value objections that impact on the public's right to know and law enforcement. Can you trivialize your opponent's arguments? Can you maximize your own? Without researching the arguments, how can you maintain that privacy is the most important right.

6. Identify three independent reasons why increasing resources for the drug war is justified. Is there any overlap among your claims? Could the opposition think of any way to link your reasons together? How would you keep them independent?

6

Roles of the Speaker

Chapter Outline

Key Terms

construction
concession
refutation
repetition
extension
prima facie case
transitions
negative position statement
add-ons
grouping arguments
Lincoln-Douglas debate

In every debate, certain expectations govern how the debate will proceed. In value debate, two sides debate each other. An affirmative side must defend the resolution and a negative side must deny the resolution. Two distinct formats tend to dominate academic value debate. In the Cross-Examination Debate Association format, the two sides are comprised of a team of two individuals presenting two speeches each. In the Lincoln-Douglas format, the two sides are comprised of one individual each who presents all of the speeches for a side.

Regardless of format, all debates consist of two distinct types of speeches: constructive speeches, where each side outlines its positions, and rebuttal speeches, where each side extends and summarizes its positions. The affirmative has the first and last speeches. This structure provides competitive fairness, given that the affirmative team also has the burden of proving that the resolution should be affirmed.

The speeches in a debate are distinguished from one another by the combination of argumentative strategies available. In the most general sense, you have five options: you can construct arguments, concede arguments, refute arguments, repeat arguments, and extend arguments. Each speech allows you a particular combination of these strategies, with certain conventions requiring some options and prohibiting others.

Construction involves the initiation of new claims in a debate. Both affirmative and negative debaters have an opportunity to present the arguments that they feel will win them the debate. Construction of an argument should involve a label specifying the argument, some supporting evidence to sustain the claim, and some reasoning to explain the importance of the argument within the entire debate context.

Concession is failure by a member of either team to answer an opposing argument. If you fail to respond to an argument, you "drop" or concede the argument. Sometimes, debaters concede arguments intentionally. As the previous chapter on analyzing the interaction among arguments indicates, conceding one argument can allow a team to capitalize on other arguments in the debate. At other times, debaters will concede arguments unintentionally. They may forget that the original argument existed or they may simply not have time to respond. Regardless of the reason for conceding the argument, the other team always wins the argument and can use the claim to whatever benefit it can.

You may also respond to an argument by refuting the argument directly. **Refutation** is the process of denying the reasoning of an opponent's argument. We have already described how to analyze the data, warrant, and claim that constitute an argument (see Chapter Six of the core text). We have also explained how to analyze the validity of evidentiary support for an argument (see Chapter Five, core text). Finally, we have described several lines of argument for refuting the general lines of argument for value debate (see Chapters Two through Four of this text). Refutation is an attempt to disprove your opponent's claim through these options.

At times, debaters use **repetition** of arguments previously made in a debate. If one team concedes an argument, for example, a debater from the other team might repeat the original argument and explain why winning this argument would help win the debate. Repetition of the label of an argument can alert the debate judge to what argument is under discussion. At times, however, repetition can be harmful to a debater. If a debater's opponent responds to an original argument, repetition of that argument would be equivalent to conceding the point. Debaters should not confuse repetition of an argument with answering objections offered by the opponent.

When you answer your opponent's response, you should extend your argument rather than repeat your initial argument. **Extension** elaborates on the original point by either directly clashing with arguments against the original point, or by expanding the scope of the original argument.

An example will help illustrate the difference between repetition and extension in a debate. Karin might argue that television cameras in criminal courts impede justice. Tariq, Karin's opponent, might respond that television news coverage of criminal trials is no worse than newspaper coverage. If Karin merely repeats that cameras impede justice, she would concede the argument to Tariq. Instead, Karin could extend the argument by indicating that television news is always more sensational than the printed word. Because television news condenses a trial into a few pictures, it sensationalizes a trial much more than a newspaper or magazine article. In this way, Karin extends the original argument—that cameras impede justice—by blunting Tariq's claim that television is no worse than newspapers.

Karin can also extend arguments by elaborating on the original argument. Karin could extend the argument that cameras impede justice by noting that attorneys and judges play to the cameras. By playing to the cameras, they distort the courtroom proceedings. Note, however, that Karin would still have to respond to Tariq's argument that television is not worse than newspapers. Merely repeating the original argument that cameras impede justice would not help Karin's position, since Tariq has answered the more general argument already.

We examine how the five argumentative strategies (construction, concession, refutation, repetition, and extension) interact within each speech of the debate in the remaining two sections of this chapter. In the first section of this chapter, we discuss the conventions and options for the speeches in team debate. In the second, we discuss the conventions and options for the speeches in Lincoln-Douglas debate.

Team Debate Format

In team debate, each individual must give two speeches: one constructive and one rebuttal speech. Conventional debate practices specify the order and time limits for these speeches. Unless indicated otherwise (classroom time limits frequently require adjustment), the order and length of the speeches will be:

	Time Limits
First Affirmative Constructive	8 minutes
First Negative Constructive	8 minutes
Second Affirmative Constructive	8 minutes
Second Negative Constructive	8 minutes
First Negative Rebuttal	5 minutes
First Affirmative Rebuttal	5 minutes
Second Negative Rebuttal	5 minutes
Second Affirmative Rebuttal	5 minutes

First Affirmative Constructive

The first affirmative constructive is limited to the argumentative strategy of construction. Absent any other arguments in the debate, the first affirmative constructive must initiate entirely new arguments throughout the speech. This speech attempts to construct a **prima facie case,** i.e., one that on its face presents a reasoned argument for the resolution. In order to structure a prima facie case, the affirmative should present the three general lines of value debate: definition (or topicality), criteria, and justification. Ordinarily, definitions are explicitly stated. At times, the affirmative implicitly defines terms when establishing criteria and justifying a value. With the three lines of argument, the affirmative should provide supporting evidence to prove that the resolution is probably true. The strategies for initiating and supporting these lines of argument have been fully discussed in earlier chapters of this book and in your core text.

Strategically, the affirmative has numerous options for constructing the affirmative case. As Chapter Five on analyzing interaction between arguments indicated, including certain arguments can encourage your opponent to present contradictory, irrelevant, or trivial arguments. When constructing a first affirmative speech, you should consider how you want the debate to look at the end of the debate. The decision to include or exclude a given argument can improve or diminish your competitive chances by the end of the debate.

In order to organize the affirmative case into a persuasive justification of the resolution, the first affirmative constructive should arrange the lines of argument carefully. There are several options, leaving the choice of how best to present the material to the affirmative team. The affirmative team should choose the most persuasive and strategically sound organization pattern for its specific arguments. The conventional format organizational structure looks like the following:

Resolved: that the American judicial system has overemphasized freedom of the press.

I. Definition of the resolution
  A. Definition of "American judicial system"
  B. Definition of "has overemphasized"
  C. Definition of "freedom of the press"

First Affirmative Constructive

I. Definition of the resolution.
   A. Definition of "American judicial system."
   B. Definition of "has overemphasized."
   C. Definition of "freedom of the press."

II. Criterion: Judicial system should maximize justice.

III. Televised criminal trials infringe on justice.
   A. Cameras exist in many criminal trials.
   B. Cameras sensationalize trials.
   C. Sensational reporting infringes on justice.

Figure 6.1 Case Flowsheet after First Affirmative Constructive

II. Criterion: Judicial system should maximize justice.
III. Televised criminal trials infringe on justice.
    A. Cameras exist in many criminal trials.
    B. Cameras sensationalize trials.
    C. Sensational reporting infringes on justice.

You may find another affirmative structure that will more persuasively present your case. After you have outlined the first affirmative constructive, you are ready to write the first affirmative speech. Unlike the other speeches in the debate that are given extemporaneously, the first affirmative constructive is a manuscript. As a manuscripted speech, it offers you an opportunity to make a strong, clear argument for the judge's consideration.

In wording the speech, use the most powerful language possible. Phrases that convey precise meaning are essential. Efficient use of language ensures that you make the point in the least amount of time. The first affirmative constructive offers an excellent opportunity to frame your arguments in the most efficient way possible because it is written in advance of the debate. You should use our previously discussed strategies for power wording the first affirmative constructive (see Chapter Seven of the core text).

Transitions are often overlooked in first affirmative constructives. Transitional statements provide a bridge between one argument and the next. In many speeches, they are included as afterthoughts, if at all. First affirmative constructives should have transitions between arguments, between pieces of supporting material, and where arguments and evidence come together. Proper transitions should 1) preview upcoming arguments or claims made in the context of supporting material; 2) connect one idea to the following one by indicating the logic of the speech's organizational structure; and 3) show the importance of an argument or evidentiary claim to the overall persuasive case for change. Strong transitions can present a coherent picture for a judge struggling to make sense of a myriad of arguments and evidenced claims.

A properly argued, strategically constructed, and well-worded first affirmative constructive can be invaluable to affirmative debaters. A strong speech can provide a reference point for all the arguments in the debate. The speech should begin preempting likely attacks by the negative and should leave no doubt that the affirmative meets the prima facie burdens (topicality, criteria, and justification). If the speech accomplishes these goals, it represents a persuasive case for affirming the resolution.

First Negative Constructive

Like the first affirmative constructive, the first negative constructive formulates new arguments in the debate. As the first speaker representing the team opposed to the resolution, the first negative constructive introduces many of the arguments that form the negative attack. But unlike the first affirmative, the first negative constructive can concede and refute arguments in the debate. If part of

First Affirmative Constructive	First Negative Constructive
	Regulated access in the courtroom can ensure justice and protect freedom of the press.
I. Definition of the resolution. A. Definition of "American judicial system." B. Definition of "has overemphasized." C. Definition of "freedom of the press."	
II. Criterion: Judicial system should maximize justice.	1. Free press is a more important value than individual justice.
III. Televised criminal trials infringe on justice. A. Cameras exist in many criminal trials. B. Cameras sensationalize trials. C. Sensational reporting infringes on justice.	1. Regulations can minimize effects of the camera.

Figure 6.2 Case Flowsheet after First Negative Constructive

the first affirmative constructive is blatantly true, the first negative may choose not to waste time arguing the point. The first negative may also have strategic reasons for conceding parts of the first affirmative constructive. (Debaters should refer to Chapter 5 of this volume, "Interaction Among Lines of Argument," to help identify parts of the first affirmative that are likely to create tensions with other arguments in the debate.) The first negative constructive will want to refute the remaining claims of the first affirmative constructive to prevent them from becoming winning arguments for the affirmative.

To illuminate the first negative constructive, let's return to our first affirmative constructive on televised criminal trials. This sample debate demonstrates the three conventional responsibilities of the first negative constructive.

Introduce the Negative Position

A **negative position statement** is an overview that encompasses all the negative arguments in the debate and establishes an argumentative tie between them. If the negative's plan of attack is consistent and well considered, some theme should emerge as the guiding philosophy of all negative arguments. In our debate, Tariq says in the negative position statement that "regulated access in the courtroom can ensure justice and protect freedom of the press." The position clearly encompasses the other negative arguments presented. If justice can be accommodated, as Tariq claims, then it is not necessary to choose between press freedom and justice as implied in the resolution. Tariq's philosophy would sustain rejection of the resolution if he wins his arguments. The negative also highlights the negative countervalue that freedom of the press is important.

A good position statement not only encompasses all of the negative arguments, it also magnifies the impact of arguments beyond what they would have separately. In our debate, the negative presents the judge with a choice: either support a value that compromises a free press or support the regulation that accommodates justice *and* a free press. The negative, in this instance, does not have to win each separate argument, but each argument that the negative does win heightens the rationale for rejecting the resolution.

Refute First Affirmative Arguments

The first negative constructive should initiate arguments that undermine the affirmative's topicality, criteria, and justification. (See Chapters Two, Three, and Four of this volume for arguments that deny these three general lines of argument.) You can choose to attack the argument, the evidence used to support the argument, or both. While an attack on each line of argument is not essential, the first negative constructive has the option of initiating arguments against each one. If you are not certain where the affirmative's case is weak, you may want to attack all parts of the case to ensure some options later in the debate. In the debate between Karin and Tariq, Tariq refutes the criteria by indicating that a free press is more important than individual justice and refutes the justification by arguing that the effects of the camera can be minimized by acceptable regulation.

The first negative needs to remember that concession is also an option when attacking the affirmative case. The negative only has to win one of the three general lines of argument to win the debate. Consequently, it may be to your advantage to have the first negative constructive concede 1) affirmative claims that the affirmative seems certain to win; 2) claims that force responses that contradict your other arguments in the debate; or 3) claims that enhance some or all of your arguments in the debate. In this debate, Tariq elects to concede the definitions to Karin in order to spare time to construct or refute other important arguments.

Construct Abbreviated Countervalue and Topicality Arguments

Up until a few years ago, first negative constructive speeches rarely mentioned countervalue arguments. Recently, the advantage of discovering the affirmative's responses to value objections early in the debate has prompted many first negatives to initiate shortened versions of these arguments. The abbreviated form is necessary because the first negative constructive has so many other important responsibilities. The abbreviated form of a countervalue consists of a quick explanation of why the countervalue trades off with the resolution and of the importance, or impact, of the argument. Tariq presents two value objections in the debate with Karin: 1) restricting cameras from the courtroom violates the First Amendment; and 2) crime control is more important than justice.

The reasons the negative may choose to develop short versions of topicality arguments are the same reasons the negative may choose to develop shortened versions of plan attacks. The time pressures produced by the other responsibilities of the first negative preclude lengthy versions of these arguments. Nevertheless, eliciting affirmative responses to the topicality argument is a good reason to place a shortened version of a topicality argument in the first negative constructive. The abbreviated topicality argument should include 1) the violation of topicality committed by the affirmative; 2) an alternative definition of terms offered by the negative; 3) the standard that should determine if a legitimate violation exists; and 4) the impact of the topicality argument.

By the end of the first negative constructive, the speaker should have constructed the bulk of the negative's arguments, at least in an abbreviated form. A strategic first negative presents a coherent structure that will ultimately provide a frame for assessing all the arguments in the debate.

Second Affirmative Constructive

The second affirmative constructive is the first speaker in the debate who has all five strategies for argument development available. The second affirmative constructive *constructs* new arguments that will enhance the affirmative's position in the debate, *concedes* negative arguments that are true or that prompt contradiction, *refutes* arguments that might be threatening to the affirmative position, *repeats* arguments unanswered by the first negative, and *extends* original arguments to bypass the negative attack. Generally, the second affirmative constructive is attempting to accomplish four goals with this speech.

First Affirmative Constructive	First Negative Constructive
	Counter value objections:
	I. Restricting access violates the First Amendment.
	II. Crime control outweighs justice.

Figure 6.2   (Cont.) Off-case Flowsheet after First Negative Constructive

Rebuild the Affirmative Case

From the first sentences of the second affirmative constructive, you should present a strong overall reason for asking the judge to affirm the resolution. Usually this involves responding to the negative's position statement, perhaps turning it to the affirmative's advantage. In the debate between Karin and Tariq, Karin points out that the paramount objective of the court system is to ensure a just verdict, and that the press can report the proceeding of a trial without television cameras. Both justice and a free press can be accommodated, then, if cameras are excluded from the courtroom. The second affirmative constructive needs a simple statement or two to rebuild the rationale for the affirmative case. This opening statement should place the affirmative on the offensive from the beginning of the speech.

Answer First Negative Arguments

The second affirmative constructive is responsible for answering each argument presented in the first negative constructive. The second affirmative can choose to extend, refute, or concede an argument, but failure to respond will result in the negative winning the argument.

Karin extends the criteria and justification arguments outlined in the first affirmative constructive. By taking this step, she improves her chances of defeating Tariq's arguments. Karin responds to the negative claim that freedom of the press is more important than the needs of justice by noting that the press, through its coverage, often demands that justice be served. She extends her initial claim that the principles of justice are more important by indicating that a press willing to forfeit justice does not justify the same degree of freedom and protection that we normally assign to the press. Karin also responds to Tariq's claim that restrictions on television cameras can minimize any adverse effects on justice by arguing that restricted coverage can be even more sensational. Restricted access leaves the media with no choice but to cover any sensational aspects that the attorneys and judges want to introduce into the trial for their own political gain. Karin concludes that restricting cameras might minimize some forms of distraction, but not enough to preserve justice.

Karin also refutes the countervalues constructed in the first negative speech. She argues that restrictions on the cameras that Tariq proposes would also violate freedom of the press. Karin also argues that other forms of reporting preserve the value of freedom of the press, fulfilling the public's right to know. Against Tariq's objection that justice compromises crime control, Karin argues that ensuring a just verdict does not hurt crime control efforts. She also insists that justice is more important than crime control. Finally, she claims that allowing cameras in the courtroom would harm crime control because the publicity would discourage potential witnesses from coming forward to testify.

First Affirmative Constructive	First Negative Constructive	Second Affirmative Constructive
	Regulated access in the courtroom can ensure justice and protect freedom of the press.	Paramount function of the court system is to ensure a just verdict. The press can report on a trial without cameras.
I. Definition of the resolution. A. Definition of "American judicial system." B. Definition of "has overemphasized." C. Definition of "freedom of the press."		
II. Criteria: Judicial system should maximize justice.	1. Free press is a more important value than individual justice.	1. Justice is the primary purpose of government.
		2. Press coverage demands justice.
		3. A press willing to forfeit justice does not deserve the same protection.
III. Televised criminal trials infringe on justice. A. Cameras exist in many criminal trials. B. Cameras sensationalize trials. C. Sensational reporting infringes on justice.	1. Regulations can minimize effects of the camera.	1. Restrictions force coverage to be sensationalistic.
		2. Restrictions might minimize some distractions, but not enough to preserve justice.
		Add-on: Privacy Television cameras cause violations of the right to privacy because they publicize the case.

Figure 6.3   Case Flowsheet after Second Affirmative Constructive

In all our examples from the debate between Karin and Tariq, the attacks have focused on the *claims* offered by both sides. Debaters should also feel free to attack the *evidence* used to support the claims in a debate. (For lines of argument useful for refuting evidence, see Chapter Five of the core text.)

When refuting each argument presented by the first negative and extending important arguments offered by the first affirmative, you should work within the organizational framework of the first affirmative constructive. If you merely answer the first negative attack with no reference to the first affirmative constructive, the result will be a defensive speech that would leave the impression that you are on the run. Instead, you should repeat the label of each first affirmative contention and paraphrase the original supporting evidence. Only then should you, as the second affirmative constructive speaker, quickly refer to the negative's arguments related to the point and offer the affirmative response. By using this approach, you will remember arguments dropped by the negative team and possible answers to the negative arguments incorporated into the structure of the first affirmative constructive.

Construct Additional Justifications

The second affirmative constructive has the option to present additional reasoning for why the judge should affirm the resolution. Because this speech is the last opportunity the affirmative will have to construct new arguments, the second affirmative constructive frequently spends some time presenting additional justification. The additional reasons are sometimes called **add-ons** for short. Karin offers one add-on in the debate with Tariq. Karin maintains that televised trials violate the privacy of defendants. If defendants have their cases heard on the television news, they will lose important rights of privacy. Privacy of both defendants and victims goes unprotected when cameras are in the courtroom.

Preempt Second Negative Attacks

In some debates, negative debaters will save some of the most difficult arguments for the affirmative until the second negative constructive. The reason for this is that the affirmative speaker following the second negative constructive has only about half the time that the second affirmative has to answer arguments. As a result, the second affirmative constructive may want to anticipate arguments that the negative will be making in the debate. Certainly, this strategy has the potential to backfire. You could make several arguments to an anticipated negative attack, and the negative could choose not to initiate that argument. Nevertheless, if the affirmative has a weakness that takes time to explain away, the second affirmative constructive may choose to preempt negative argumentation.

Second Negative Constructive

The second negative constructive is the only other speech in the debate that allows the speaker to use all five argument development strategies. The second negative constructive is the last opportunity that the negative has to initiate new

First Affirmative Constructive	First Negative Constructive	Second Affirmative Constructive
	Counter value objections:	
	I. Restricting access violates the First Amendment.	1. Regulations proposed by the negative also violate the freedom of the press.
		2. Other forms of reporting fulfill the reason for free press—the right to know.
	II. Crime control outweighs justice.	1. A just verdict does not harm crime control.
		2. Justice outweighs crime control.
		3. Cameras hurt crime control because witnesses are afraid to testify.

Figure 6.3 (Cont.) Off-case Flowsheet after Second Affirmative Constructive

arguments into the debate. The speaker can concede, repeat, or extend arguments in the debate as they benefit the negative team. The second negative constructive does not want to attempt to answer all affirmative arguments in the debate. The reason for this is "the negative block." At this point in the debate, the negative has two speeches in a row: the second negative constructive and the first negative rebuttal. If the second negative constructive attempts to answer all the arguments in the debate, the first negative rebuttal will be wasted. Strategically, the negative speakers should divide the affirmative arguments to maximize the number and quality of responses they can provide.

In our debate, Tariq chooses to refute the add-on presented in the second affirmative constructive and the two value objections, leaving arguments related to the remaining general lines of argument to the first negative rebuttal. When structuring the second negative constructive, the speaker should consider four responsibilities.

Extend the Negative Position

Like the other speakers, the second negative constructive should start on the offensive. Coordinating with the first negative constructive's position statement, the second negative constructive can extend the negative's philosophy toward the issues in the debate. In this debate, Tariq extends the original position statement, arguing that a free press should be accommodated when justice can be preserved. He reconstructs the position to offer a way of weighing the arguments. He argues that a free press can ensure that the criminal court system will be more just if it is accountable in the popular press. Highlighting the potential for a free press to ensure justice, Tariq frames the negative arguments as the superior method of resolving conflict between justice and a free press.

Construct New Value Objections or Case Attacks

Ordinarily, the second negative constructive spends the bulk of the speaking time raising value objections. In our debate, Tariq feels the negative already has too many arguments to address to spend time on additional value objections. As a result, he devotes his time to extending previously presented value objections. If the first negative constructive is not able or chooses not to respond to an argument that is critical to the affirmative's case, the second negative constructive is the last opportunity the negative has to respond to the point. Therefore, the second negative constructive must be sufficiently flexible to ensure that no major arguments by the affirmative go unanswered into the rebuttal speeches.

Had a threatening affirmative argument remained unanswered, Tariq would have had to refute the argument in the second negative constructive. He could not allow the argument to remain unanswered going into the rebuttal speeches or it would be too late. As we stated in the beginning of this chapter, new arguments are not permissible in rebuttals. Refutation of previously unanswered arguments is equivalent to presenting a new argument and is illegitimate. You must be certain that you respond to all affirmative

First Affirmative Constructive	First Negative Constructive	Second Affirmative Constructive	Second Negative Constructive
	Regulated access in the courtroom can ensure justice and protect freedom of the press.	Paramount function of the court system is to ensure a just verdict. The press can report on a trial without cameras.	Free press should be protected when justice can be preserved. Also, a free press means an accountable justice system.
I. Definition of the resolution. A. Definition of "American judicial system." B. Definition of "has overemphasized." C. Definition of "freedom of the press."			
II. Criteria: Judicial system should maximize justice.	1. Free press is a more important value than individual justice.	1. Justice is the primary purpose of government.	
		2. Press coverage demands justice.	
		3. A press willing to forfeit justice does not deserve the same protection.	
III. Televised criminal trials infringe on justice. A. Cameras exist in many criminal trials. B. Cameras sensationalize trials. C. Sensational reporting infringes on justice.	1. Regulations can minimize effects of the camera.	1. Restrictions force coverage to be sensationalistic. 2. Restrictions might minimize some distractions, but not enough to preserve justice.	
		Add-on: Privacy Television cameras cause violations of the right to privacy because they publicize the case.	1. Privacy is irrelevant, it is not related to the criteria in the debate. 2. Freedom of the press outweighs privacy.

Figure 6.4 Case Flowsheet after Second Negative Constructive

constructive positions not addressed by the first negative constructive by the conclusion of the second negative constructive, or recognize that the affirmative will win the arguments left unanswered.

Answer Affirmative Responses to Critical Negative Attacks

With the longest speech remaining for the negative team, the second negative constructive speaker should extend arguments by the negative that are critical to opposing the resolution. This requires refuting arguments that the negative debaters are losing that could cost them the debate or extending arguments that might ultimately win them the debate.

In the debate between Tariq and Karin, Tariq extends the two countervalues presented in the first negative constructive. He begins by responding to the affirmative answers to the two arguments. Tariq chooses to extend the countervalue of a free press because he believes that it is the most important argument for the negative in this specific debate. Determined to win the debate on the argument that a free press is the most important value in the debate, Tariq refutes each of the affirmative answers to the value objection.

Tariq refutes the affirmative answer that a free press is protected by other forms of reporting. Other forms of reporting do not justify restricting television news media. Even if other forms of reporting can cover trials, television is a unique means of communicating the news. Television news is more powerful than other forms of media coverage. Tariq refutes Karin's claim that other regulations violate the free press in two ways. First, one bad regulation does not justify two bad regulations. That is the kind of logic that erodes a free press. Second, television is a more powerful medium than others, so television news should not be restricted.

In this debate, Tariq clearly believes that the First Amendment argument is a potentially winning argument in the debate. As a good second negative constructive speaker, he extends the importance of the argument to the debate. Rather than merely moving on to the next argument, he offers support for the claim that press is necessary for the just operation of government, including the courts. By taking this step, Tariq magnifies the issue in the context of the debate and increases the chances that the negative team will win.

Tariq also chooses to concede the argument that crime control is more important than justice. The decision is a good one because the affirmative responses to the argument could turn the argument into an affirmative justification of the value. If cameras discourage witnesses from coming forward, then cameras do not increase crime control. Instead, Tariq concedes that crime is not an important issue in the debate. He concedes Karin's claim that criminal procedure has no effect on crime. And, to help make sure that the affirmative cannot claim the argument, he indicates that cameras in the courtroom increase the severity of sentencing in some trials.

First Affirmative Constructive	First Negative Constructive	Second Affirmative Constructive	Second Negative Constructive
	Counter value objections:		
	I. Restricting access violates the First Amendment.	1. Regulations proposed by the negative also violate the freedom of the press.	1. One ban does not justify another. 2. Television is a more powerful medium and shouldn't be regulated.
		2. Other forms of reporting fulfill the reason for free press—the right to know.	1. Other forms do not justify violations of the freedom of the press. 2. Television is a unique way of communicating news. 3. Freedom of the press is necessary for just operation of government.
	II. Crime control outweighs justice.	1. A just verdict does not harm crime control. 2. Justice outweighs crime control. 3. Cameras hurt crime control because witnesses are afraid to testify.	1. Concede the crime position. 2. Crime is not important. 3. Grant #1: justice is irrelevant to crime. 4. Cameras increase the severity of punishment and thus decrease crime.

Figure 6.4   (Cont.) Off-case Flowsheet after Second Negative Constructive

Respond to Additional Justifications

Usually, the second negative constructive has the responsibility to answer any additional justifications presented in the second affirmative constructive. Having the time allotted to a constructive speech, the second negative constructive has more time to develop the negative's responses to new justifications than does the first negative rebuttal. The options available for answering an add-on are identical to those appropriate for responding to the first affirmative constructive. Is the justification topical? Does it meet the criteria? Can competing values outweigh the add-on? In response to Karin's privacy add-on, Tariq maintains that privacy is an unimportant right. Tariq also argues that the add-on has no relationship to the criterion that justice is paramount. Therefore, there is no way to compare the value of privacy in this debate. Finally, Tariq argues that a free press is more important than privacy.

Because the second negative constructive is the last constructive speech in the debate, it is your last opportunity to construct new arguments. The second negative constructive speaker must have a strong overall picture of what is occurring in the debate. Where are new responses needed to ensure a negative victory? Will constructing new negative plan attacks place a larger burden on the affirmative rebuttalists? The second negative should allocate time for presenting arguments in accordance with strategic benefits to the negative team.

First Negative Rebuttal

In the first negative rebuttal, you have four options for developing arguments. You can concede, repeat, refute arguments presented in the second affirmative constructive, or extend arguments presented in the first negative constructive. Like all the rebuttalists in the debate, the first negative rebuttalist cannot construct new arguments. New arguments are forbidden in the rebuttal speeches to ensure that the debate remains narrow enough so that the debaters can resolve existing issues. Sometimes the notion of "no new arguments in the rebuttal" can be confusing to beginning debaters. The key is to distinguish between new arguments and extensions or refutations. If the second affirmative initiates a new argument, the first negative rebuttalist can refute the claim. However, constructing a new value objection or new case attack against issues introduced in the first affirmative constructive are illegitimate. The first negative constructive has three argumentative responsibilities.

Extend Attacks Against the General Lines of Argument

The first negative rebuttal attempts to further the original attacks made against the affirmative's definition, criteria, and justification. This requires the first negative rebuttalist not only to answer the affirmative responses, but to explain why the negative's claims are stronger than the affirmative's claims. As an example, Tariq would want to extend the argument against Karin's argument that justice is the ultimate purpose of government. Tariq might undermine the affirmative extension that justice is the primary purpose by arguing that government has many

First Affirmative Constructive	First Negative Constructive	Second Affirmative Constructive	Second Negative Constructive
	Regulated access in the courtroom can ensure justice and protect freedom of the press.	Paramount function of the court system is to ensure a just verdict. The press can report on a trial without cameras.	Free press should be protected when justice can be preserved. Also, a free press means an accountable justice system.
I. Definition of the resolution. A. Definition of "American judicial system." B. Definition of "has overemphasized." C. Definition of "freedom of the press."			
II. Criteria: Judicial system should maximize justice.	1. Free press is a more important value than individual justice.	1. Justice is the primary purpose of government.	
		2. Press coverage demands justice.	
		3. A press willing to forfeit justice does not deserve the same protection.	
III. Televised criminal trials infringe on justice. A. Cameras exist in many criminal trials. B. Cameras sensationalize trials. C. Sensational reporting infringes on justice.	1. Regulations can minimize effects of the camera.	1. Restrictions force coverage to be sensationalistic.	
		2. Restrictions might minimize some distractions, but not enough to preserve justice.	
		Add-on: Privacy Television cameras cause violations of the right to privacy because they publicize the case.	1. Privacy is irrelevant; it is not related to the criteria in the debate.
			2. Freedom of the press outweighs privacy.

Figure 6.5 Case Flowsheet after First Negative Rebuttal

1. There are many
   purposes for
   government, and a
   free press checks an
   abusive government.

2. Free press outweighs
   the purpose of
   government.

1. Concede; this proves
   a free press should
   be protected to
   ensure justice.

1. Impeachment and
   dismissal solve
   injustice and camera
   mugging.

purposes. In our system the purpose of government is to ensure freedom for all, and a completely free press is necessary to check the power of government. As a result, when the value of a free press competes with the purposes of government, a free press is more important.

In addition to answering the affirmative response, Tariq indicates the impact of his argument on the debate. He argues that a free press is necessary to prevent abuses of the justice system. Tariq concedes Karin's argument that the press itself values justice. It is because the press insists upon justice that a free press is necessary in a free society. Finally, Tariq extends his responses to the justification of the value by arguing that justice can still be preserved if judges can be impeached, decisions appealed, and attorneys cited for contempt.

When extending arguments made against the three general lines of argument, the first negative rebuttalist has a number of options. Throughout this text, we have outlined arguments used to resolve topicality, criteria, and justification claims (see Chapters Two, Three, and Four). Additionally, first negative rebuttalists can indicate why the evidence they use in support of their claims is superior to that of the affirmative (see Chapter Five of the core text).

Focus the Debate on Issues the Negative Is Winning

With only a small amount of time in the rebuttal speech, you want to spend the bulk of your speech time extending arguments that the negative is winning. As the first negative rebuttalist, you must be able to distinguish between those arguments the negative is losing that are *unimportant* to the outcome of the debate and those arguments that must be extended for the negative to win the debate. Recognizing and conceding losing issues that will not cost the negative team the debate is a critical skill for an effective first negative rebuttalist. Tariq realizes that the negative has no analytical or evidenced responses to the argument that the press demands justice. Therefore, he should concede the argument and focus attention on how the argument substantiates the negative position. If he can use the fact that the press demands justice to enhance his position, the concession is more powerful.

Aid Second Negative in Coverage of Important Arguments

At times, the second negative constructive will not succeed in laying out all of the negative team's answers to important issues in the debate. When this occurs, the first negative rebuttalist should be willing to help. If the second negative constructive has not had time to respond to the affirmative's add-on about privacy, for example, the first negative rebuttalist should use a portion of the speech to make sure that the argument has a sufficient response. Again, the first negative rebuttalist can answer arguments presented in the second affirmative constructive, even if the second negative constructive does not respond, or "drops," the affirmative answers. If the second negative constructive and the first negative rebuttalist fail to respond to an argument before the first affirmative rebuttalist extends the argument, the affirmative will win the issue. Debaters reluctant to view the entire debate as a team effort will lose debates because they do not compensate for each individual debater's weaknesses.

The first negative rebuttalist wants to place as much pressure as possible on the next speaker, who must respond to both the second negative constructive and the first negative rebuttal within the time limit of a rebuttal speech. If the first negative rebuttalist can extend, rather than repeat the constructive arguments, this speaker can play a key role in undermining the affirmative's chances in the debate.

First Affirmative Rebuttal

Like the first negative rebuttalist, the first affirmative rebuttalist can concede, refute, repeat, or extend arguments in the debate. But the argumentative responsibilities of the first affirmative rebuttalist are much broader than those of the first negative rebuttalist. The first affirmative rebuttalist has to respond to all of the arguments that can win the debate for the negative. To achieve this monumental task, this speaker should identify similar arguments so that they can be answered by their common weakness (this is sometimes referred to as **grouping arguments**). Additionally, the first affirmative rebuttalist will want to de-emphasize unimportant arguments, read little evidence or read efficiently phrased evidence, emphasize word economy, speak more rapidly than other speakers, and minimize the transitions used when moving from point to point. As much as possible, the first affirmative rebuttalist should accomplish the following objectives.

Refute New Arguments Made in Second Negative Constructive

Because the affirmative has had no prior opportunity to respond to these arguments, the first affirmative rebuttalist usually answers new second negative arguments at the beginning of the speech. This speaker can deny the negative claims, minimize their force in the debate, or turn them into additional reasons for why the affirmative should win the debate.

In the debate between Tariq and Karin, Tariq did not argue a new value objection in the second negative constructive. Had he done so, this would have been the first opportunity the affirmative had to respond to the argument. The first affirmative rebuttalist is allowed, in fact, *required* to refute the new arguments raised in the second negative constructive. Because these are direct responses to opposing argumentation and the first affirmative rebuttal is the first time affirmative has had a chance to answer, they are not new arguments.

Extend Answers to Important Negative Arguments

In our debate, Tariq has argued two value objections (free press and crime control). Each of these arguments potentially outweighs any significant justification the affirmative may win in the debate. If the affirmative debaters lose any of these arguments, they stand to lose the debate. Considering the important negative arguments, Karin realizes that there is only one countervalue objection to

First Affirmative Constructive	First Negative Constructive	Second Affirmative Constructive	Second Negative Constructive
	Regulated access in the courtroom can ensure justice and protect freedom of the press.	Paramount function of the court system is to ensure a just verdict. The press can report on a trial without cameras.	Free press should be protected when justice can be preserved. Also, a free press means an accountable justice system.
I. Definition of the resolution. A. Definition of "American judicial system." B. Definition of "has overemphasized." C. Definition of "freedom of the press."			
II. Criteria: Judicial system should maximize justice.	1. Free press is a more important value than individual justice.	1. Justice is the primary purpose of government.	
		2. Press coverage demands justice. 3. A press willing to forfeit justice does not deserve the same protection.	
III. Televised criminal trials infringe on justice. A. Cameras exist in many criminal trials. B. Cameras sensationalize trials. C. Sensational reporting infringes on justice.	1. Regulations can minimize effects of the camera.	1. Restrictions force coverage to be sensationalistic. 2. Restrictions might minimize some distractions, but not enough to preserve justice.	
		Add-on: Privacy Television cameras cause violations of the right to privacy because they publicize the case.	1. Privacy is irrelevant; it is not related to the criteria in the debate. 2. Freedom of the press outweighs privacy.

Figure 6.6 Case Flowsheet after First Affirmative Rebuttal

First Negative Rebuttal	First Affirmative Rebuttal

1. There are many purposes for government, and a free press checks an abusive government.

2. Free press outweighs the purpose of government.

1. Concede; this proves a free press should be protected to ensure justice.

1. Justice is still important even if a free press helps to ensure that the justice system works. Consider which side furthers justice more.

1. Impeachment and dismissal solve injustice and camera mugging.

1. Television coverage can still distort trial proceedings because pictures are more sensational.

2. Only television is powerful enough to disrupt justice.

1. Protecting privacy ensures justice by allowing witnesses to testify.

First Affirmative Constructive	First Negative Constructive	Second Affirmative Constructive	Second Negative Constructive
	Counter value objections:		
	I. Restricting access violates the First Amendment.	1. Regulations proposed by the negative also violate the freedom of the press.	1. One ban does not justify another. 2. Television is a more powerful medium and shouldn't be regulated.
		2. Other forms of reporting fulfill the reason for free press—the right to know.	1. Other forms do not justify violations of the freedom of the press. 2. Television is a unique means of communicating news. 3. Freedom of the press is necessary for just operation of government.
	II. Crime control outweighs justice.	1. A just verdict does not harm crime control. 2. Justice outweighs crime control. 3. Cameras hurt crime control because witnesses are afraid to testify.	1. Concede the crime position. 2. Crime is not important. 3. Grant #1: justice is irrelevant to crime. 4. Cameras increase the severity of punishment and thus decrease crime.

Figure 6.6   (Cont.) Off-case Flowsheet after First Affirmative Rebuttal

First Negative Rebuttal	First Affirmative Rebuttal
	1. Restricting one form of the media does not restrict the public's right to know.
	2. Entertainment value and power are irrelevant; other methods exist to inform the public.
	1. Conceded by the negative, but remember that cameras still stop witnesses from coming forward.

consider against the value of justice. The free press argument is the only argument Tariq is extending to weigh against the value of justice.

Karin begins by noting that the negative has conceded the crime control argument. But Karin reminds the judge that cameras in the courtroom discourage witnesses from coming forward. Tariq also concedes this argument and Karin believes she can use this argument to her benefit. Always pay attention to how you can use conceded arguments.

Karin also needs to extend the answers to the free press countervalue. Karin chooses to extend her second argument that other forms of reporting ensure the press is not injured by restricting television cameras. While restrictions on all media might stifle news, restricting one form of coverage does not restrict information from the public. Television reports can describe the trial. The newspapers can write about it. Karin elects to concede that television is more powerful, but argues that the purpose of the news media is to provide information, not entertain the public. Other methods of reporting ensure a free press.

Extend the General Lines of Argument

In this step, the first affirmative rebuttalist must respond to negative responses to the three general lines of argument. The first affirmative rebuttalist needs to be aware that by the end of the speech, the affirmative has to be winning topicality, criteria, and justification. As a result, the first affirmative rebuttalist must extend some arguments relevant to each of these claims. Concessions may be necessary because of time constraints, but the overall objective of winning each of the lines of argument is paramount.

Karin extends the criteria by noting that justice is still important even if the press helps to ensure the justice system works. Karin notes that none of Tariq's arguments disprove the importance of justice. In fact, Tariq's justification of a free press is that it ensures a just government. The question, Karin argues, is which side furthers justice more.

Karin then concedes Tariq's justification that camera mugging by attorneys and judges can be controlled. To retain the justification, she argues that television news coverage can distort a trial proceeding because pictures are more sensational than a news anchor's description of a trial. Other media, such as supermarket tabloids, lack the credibility of the nightly newscast, so only television is sufficiently powerful and sensational to disrupt justice.

Karin then extends the privacy add-on that Tariq has argued does not fulfill the criteria of justice. Karin indicates that protecting the privacy of victims and witnesses does ensure justice by increasing their willingness to testify. Karin repeats the argument from the crime control objection that Tariq has conceded or dropped. Cameras discourage witnesses, which reinforces the affirmative justification argument.

Make Selective Responses to Other Negative Arguments

Once the first affirmative rebuttalist has responded to all new arguments by the second negative constructive and to other critical case arguments, the speaker can use any remaining time to cover issues less crucial to the ultimate decision in the debate. In choosing which additional arguments should be extended, you should keep in mind the overall goal of proving that the affirmative value is more important than the negative value.

Second Negative Rebuttal

The second negative rebuttalist can concede, repeat, refute, or extend arguments, but cannot construct new arguments. The second negative rebuttal is the summary speech, explaining why the negative should win the debate. The second negative rebuttalist must provide the judge with a reason to believe that the individual arguments offered by the negative come together to deny the affirmative defense of the resolution.

The second negative rebuttalist must identify the strategic options available in light of the position taken by the first affirmative rebuttalist. What strategic options are available for Tariq in our debate? Surveying the options, several issues stand out. First, he conceded the crime control value, so that argument is not available. He also has no answer to Karin's argument that justice is more important than a free press. Tariq does, however, believe that the free press argument can prove that negating the resolution would maximize justice. He also believes that much of the affirmative justification is minimized by arguments indicating that tabloids and TV news anchors could still sensationalize trials. Believing that he has minimized the affirmative justification claims and that the free press objection better achieves justice, Tariq can proceed to make intelligent choices of which arguments to concede, repeat, refute, and extend. The second negative rebuttalist should proceed with the following arguments.

Present the Closing Statement for the Negative

The second negative rebuttalist's opening statement should provide a concise, comprehensive perspective on the arguments in the debate. The statement should encompass the remaining issues in the debate, emphasizing why they support a negation of the resolution. Tariq, for example, might begin by claiming that we cannot avoid occasional sensationalism and it is the price we pay for a free press that ensures the best chance of a just judiciary. With such a statement, he attempts to place the remaining arguments in a perspective beneficial to the negative team.

Extend a Combination of Winning Arguments for the Negative

To do this, the second negative rebuttalist must determine which set of arguments provides the negative with its best opportunity to win the debate. Then, the second negative rebuttalist must refute any affirmative responses to the set of winning arguments. Finally, this speaker must explain why the combination of arguments ensures a negative victory.

In the debate between Karin and Tariq, the primary reason offered by the negative in favor of cameras in the courtroom is to ensure a free press. The negative

First Affirmative Constructive	First Negative Constructive	Second Affirmative Constructive	Second Negative Constructive
	Regulated access in the courtroom can ensure justice and protect freedom of the press.	Paramount function of the court system is to ensure a just verdict. The press can report on a trial without cameras.	Free press should be protected when justice can be preserved. Also, a free press means an accountable justice system.
I. Definition of the resolution. A. Definition of "American judicial system." B. Definition of "has overemphasized." C. Definition of "freedom of the press."			
II. Criteria: Judicial system should maximize justice.	1. Free press is a more important value than individual justice.	1. Justice is the primary purpose of government.	
		2. Press coverage demands justice.	
		3. A press willing to forfeit justice does not deserve the same protection.	
III. Televised criminal trials infringe on justice. A. Cameras exist in many criminal trials. B. Cameras sensationalize trials. C. Sensational reporting infringes on justice.	1. Regulations can minimize effects of the camera.	1. Restrictions force coverage to be sensationalistic. 2. Restrictions might minimize some distractions, but not enough to preserve justice.	
		Add-on: Privacy Television cameras cause violations of the right to privacy because they publicize the case.	1. Privacy is irrelevant; it is not related to the criteria in the debate. 2. Freedom of the press outweighs privacy.

Figure 6.7 Case Flowsheet after Second Negative Rebuttal

First Negative Rebuttal	First Affirmative Rebuttal	Second Negative Rebuttal
		We cannot avoid occasional sensationalism and it is the price we pay for a free press that ensures the best chance of a just judiciary.
		1. It would be a new argument if the affirmative were to claim that visual representation is more sensationalistic because it is more realistic.
1. There are many purposes for government, and a free press checks an abusive government. 2. Free press outweighs the purpose of government.	1. Justice is still important even if a free press helps to ensure that the justice system works. Consider which side furthers justice more.	
1. Concede; this proves a free press should be protected to ensure justice.		
1. Impeachment and dismissal solve injustice and camera mugging.	1. Television coverage can still distort trial proceedings because pictures are more sensational. 2. Only television is powerful enough to disrupt justice.	1. The affirmative has conceded that judge and attorney behavior can be minimized. 2. Tabloids will sensationalize trials also, so cameras are not a unique harm.
	1. Protecting privacy ensures justice by allowing witnesses to testify.	1. Witnesses can go into a protection program or be disguised and have their privacy protected. 2. Tabloids could also harass witnesses as easily as television.

First Affirmative Constructive	First Negative Constructive	Second Affirmative Constructive	Second Negative Constructive
	Counter value objections:		
	I. Restricting access violates the First Amendment.	1. Regulations proposed by the negative also violate the freedom of the press.	1. One ban does not justify another. 2. Television is a more powerful medium and shouldn't be regulated.
		2. Other forms of reporting fulfill the reason for free press—the right to know.	1. Other forms do not justify violations of the freedom of the press. 2. Television is a unique means of communicating news. 3. Freedom of the press is necessary for just operation of government.
	II. Crime control outweighs justice.	1. A just verdict does not harm crime control. 2. Justice outweighs crime control. 3. Cameras hurt crime control because witnesses are afraid to testify.	1. Concede the crime position. 2. Crime is not important. 3. Grant #1: justice is irrelevant to crime. 4. Cameras increase the severity of punishment and thus decrease crime.

Figure 6.7 (Cont.) Off-case Flowsheet after Second Negative Rebuttal

First Negative Rebuttal	First Affirmative Rebuttal	Second Negative Rebuttal
		1. The affirmative has conceded that television is too important to be regulated; this means a free press is an absolute value.
	1. Restricting one form of the media does not restrict the public's right to know.	1. Pictures are a unique way of communicating.
	2. Entertainment value and power are irrelevant; other methods exist to inform the public.	1. Entertaining news increases the interest of citizens in government and thus assures justice.
	1. Conceded by the negative, but remember that cameras still stop witnesses from coming forward.	

abandoned the crime control argument to extend other arguments earlier in the debate. Limited to the free press countervalue, Tariq needs to maximize the argument's impact. He could point out that in the second negative constructive, he had argued that television was too important a medium to restrict. The first affirmative rebuttalist had conceded the point. If television is the most important medium, then other forms of coverage would not be as important. Tariq could also note that pictures are more important than written or spoken words. He could also maintain that entertaining news increases citizens' interest in their government. This is the way a free press protects justice.

Minimize Winning Affirmative Arguments

The second negative rebuttalist is attempting to convince the judge that the negative better fulfills the criteria of justice by keeping cameras in the courtroom. Having maximized the impact of the negative arguments, the next step is to minimize the claims of the opposition. Tariq would want to point out the affirmative had conceded that judges and attorney behavior can be minimized through appeals and contempt proceedings. Hoping to mitigate some of Karin's justification, he could also note that other tabloids will sensationalize trials.

Tariq could also address Karin's add-on by arguing that privacy for defendants and witnesses has little effect on justice. Witnesses can go into a protection program or have their faces and voices disguised and still have their privacy protected. The print media could harass witnesses and victims as easily as television could.

Anticipate and Refute Second Affirmative Rebuttal Responses

The second negative rebuttalist must remember that the second affirmative rebuttalist can respond to any claims made in the second negative rebuttal. Therefore, the second negative rebuttalist should anticipate how the affirmative will attempt to win the debate. Then the second negative rebuttalist should extend arguments that answer the affirmative position and refute arguments that could enhance the affirmative position.

Looking at the entire debate between Tariq and Karin, Tariq can probably anticipate that Karin will be arguing that sensationalism harms justice more than cameras can keep the system working. Since the negative's defense of a free press is that it increases justice, the focus of the second affirmative rebuttalist is predictable. How could sensationalism overwhelm the effectiveness of a free press? The second affirmative rebuttalist could argue that television is worse than the tabloids because visual representations seem more realistic. The second negative rebuttalist could alert the judge to the forthcoming new argument, reminding the judge that because the negative would not have a chance to respond, the argument is illegitimate.

Second Affirmative Rebuttal

The second affirmative rebuttal is the mirror speech to the second negative rebuttal. Like the previous speech, the second affirmative rebuttalist has the option to concede, repeat, refute, and extend arguments. The second affirmative rebuttalist cannot initiate or construct new arguments in the debate. Having the opportunity to give the last speech in the debate, the second affirmative rebuttalist should be presenting the strongest summary possible of why the affirmative is winning the debate.

How can Karin determine the strongest possible affirmative position in our debate? First, she must remember that she has to win the three general lines of argument. The negative has conceded criteria in the debate, and it never challenged the topicality of the affirmative. Karin has to worry only about winning justification. Tariq has argued that television is an important medium that portrays the operation of the court uniquely to all citizens. Karin must address this argument because Tariq argues that this important medium is necessary for justice. Karin must be certain to address these arguments and extend other arguments that may be useful to the affirmative position. An explanation of the affirmative position in the second affirmative rebuttal requires the following three practices.

Present the Closing Statement for the Affirmative

Just as the second negative rebuttal speech asks the judge to deny the resolution, the second affirmative rebuttalist should begin with a bottom-line statement that explains why the judge should affirm the resolution. It is to the affirmative's benefit if this statement somehow places the negative perspective on the debate in an unflattering framework. In other words, if possible, the second affirmative rebuttalist wants to leave the judge with the feeling that the negative framework is less desirable than the affirmative framework.

In the last speech, Tariq argued that some sensationalism is necessary to ensure justice from government. Karin might want to reframe the issue by indicating that any deprivation of justice is too much to tolerate. While Tariq only speculates about the possible effect of cameras, Karin is certain that they have sensationalized some trials. Karin argues that the resolution is true if some injustice occurs.

Maximize the Winning Affirmative Arguments

The second affirmative rebuttalist must be conscious of the need to win each of the three general lines of argument. Within that framework, the second affirmative rebuttalist should choose which arguments are most likely to be persuasive with the judge. Having made these choices, the second affirmative rebuttalist should respond to any negative arguments addressing these issues. Finally, the second affirmative rebuttalist should provide reasons why these arguments should win the debate for the affirmative.

First Affirmative Constructive	First Negative Constructive	Second Affirmative Constructive	Second Negative Constructive
	Regulated access in the courtroom can ensure justice and protect freedom of the press.	Paramount function of the court system is to ensure a just verdict. The press can report on a trial without cameras.	Free press should be protected when justice can be preserved. Also, a free press means an accountable justice system.
I. Definition of the resolution. A. Definition of "American judicial system." B. Definition of "has overemphasized." C. Definition of "freedom of the press."			
II. Criteria: Judicial system should maximize justice.	1. Free press is a more important value than individual justice.	1. Justice is the primary purpose of government.	
		2. Press coverage demands justice.	
		3. A press willing to forfeit justice does not deserve the same protection.	
III. Televised criminal trials infringe on justice. A. Cameras exist in many criminal trials. B. Cameras sensationalize trials. C. Sensational reporting infringes on justice.	1. Regulations can minimize effects of the camera.	1. Restrictions force coverage to be sensationalistic.	
		2. Restrictions might minimize some distractions, but not enough to preserve justice.	
		Add-on: Privacy Television cameras cause violations of the right to privacy because they publicize the case.	1. Privacy is irrelevant; it is not related to the criteria in the debate.
			2. Freedom of the press outweighs privacy.

Figure 6.8 Case Flowsheet after Second Affirmative Rebuttal

First Negative Rebuttal	First Affirmative Rebuttal	Second Negative Rebuttal	Second Affirmative Rebuttal
		We cannot avoid occasional sensationalism and it is the price we pay for a free press that ensures the best chance of a just judiciary.	Any deprivation of justice is too much to tolerate. The negative harm is speculative, while we are certain some trials have been sensationalized by cameras.
		1. It would be a new argument if the affirmative were to claim that visual representation is more sensationalistic because it is more realistic.	
1. There are many purposes for government, and a free press checks an abusive government.	1. Justice is still important even if a free press helps to ensure that the justice system works. Consider which side furthers justice more.		
2. Free press outweighs the purpose of government.			
1. Concede; this proves a free press should be protected to ensure justice.			
1. Impeachment and dismissal solve injustice and camera mugging.	1. Television coverage can still distort trial proceedings because pictures are more sensational.	1. The affirmative has conceded that judge and attorney behavior can be minimized.	1. While the number of problems associated with televised trials may not be as high as claimed, they still represent a sufficient reason for accepting the resolution.
	2. Only television is powerful enough to disrupt justice.	2. Tabloids will sensationalize trials also, so cameras are not a unique harm.	
	1. Protecting privacy ensures justice by allowing witnesses to testify.	1. Witnesses can go into a protection program or be disguised and have their privacy protected.	1. Cameras violate justice because they deter testimony from potential witnesses.
		2. Tabloids could also harass witnesses as easily as television.	

First Affirmative Constructive	First Negative Constructive	Second Affirmative Constructive	Second Negative Constructive
	Counter value objections:		
	I. Restricting access violates the First Amendment.	1. Regulations proposed by the negative also violate the freedom of the press.	1. One ban does not justify another. 2. Television is a more powerful medium and shouldn't be regulated.
		2. Other forms of reporting fulfill the reason for free press—the right to know.	1. Other forms do not justify violations of the freedom of the press. 2. Television is a unique means of communicating news. 3. Freedom of the press is necessary for just operation of government.
	II. Crime control outweighs justice.	1. A just verdict does not harm crime control. 2. Justice outweighs crime control. 3. Cameras hurt crime control because witnesses are afraid to testify.	1. Concede the crime position. 2. Crime is not important. 3. Grant #1: justice is irrelevant to crime. 4. Cameras increase the severity of punishment and thus decrease crime.

Figure 6.8   (Cont.) Off-case Flowsheet after Second Affirmative Rebuttal

First Negative Rebuttal	First Affirmative Rebuttal	Second Negative Rebuttal	Second Affirmative Rebuttal
		1. The affirmative has conceded that television is too important to be regulated; this means a free press is an absolute value.	
	1. Restricting one form of the media does not restrict the public's right to know	1. Pictures are a unique way of communicating.	1. There are many sources of information that can help ensure a just judiciary. Other media may not be as entertaining, but they provide the news.
	2. Entertainment value and power are irrelevant; other methods exist to inform the public.	1. Entertaining news increases the interest of citizens in government and thus assures justice.	2. If justice is sacrificed to offer entertaining news, then the purpose of the free press is not worth the price.
	1. Conceded by the negative, but remember that cameras still stop witnesses from coming forward.		

Karin could indicate that television cameras lead to sensational reporting. While the number of problems associated with televised trials may not be as high as the affirmative claimed, they still represent a sufficient reason for offering the conclusion that cameras infringe on justice. Karin could indict the negative's countervalue by indicating that, by the negative's own admission, television is a more powerful medium. Only television can have such a powerful influence on policy. The negative already conceded the criteria and topicality issues in the constructive speeches. The privacy add-on proves that cameras violate justice because they deter testimony from potential witnesses.

Minimize the Winning Negative Arguments

Second affirmative rebuttalists should realistically examine the arguments in the debate and determine the ones that they are losing. The strongest second affirmative rebuttalists can recognize when an argument is potentially troublesome and can argue persuasively that its impact is minimal.

The negative's best hope in our debate is that the free press is necessary for ensuring a smooth and just court system. After all, the negative did concede the affirmative's claim that justice is the most fundamental right. The affirmative argues that there are many sources of information that can help ensure a just judiciary. Other medias besides television might not be as entertaining, but they provide the news. If justice is sacrificed to offer entertaining news, then the purpose of the free press is not worth the price. Justice is a paramount concern. Both sides agree with that; the question is who better achieves it.

Lincoln-Douglas Debate Format

Up to this point, this chapter has concentrated on the strategies appropriate for the speeches required in team debate. Another format, **Lincoln-Douglas debate**, is a contest between individuals.

As in team debate, Lincoln-Douglas debate has some conventions you need to identify. There are fewer speeches in Lincoln-Douglas debate and the speech times vary from those in team debates. Each side has one constructive speech. The negative debater has one rebuttal and the affirmative debater has two rebuttals. As in team debate, the affirmative side opens and closes the debate. Unless otherwise specified, the speech time is:

	Time Limits
Affirmative Constructive	6 Minutes
Negative Constructive	7 Minutes
First Affirmative Rebuttal	4 Minutes
Negative Rebuttal	6 Minutes
Second Affirmative Rebuttal	3 Minutes

Because each side only has one constructive speech, there is only one opportunity for each debater to construct arguments. Therefore, both sides must be prepared to present fully constructed positions in their initial speeches. The ability to construct, concede, refute, repeat, or extend is far more constricted because there are fewer speeches than in team formats.

Affirmative Constructive

As in team debate, the affirmative constructive can only construct arguments. The speech attempts to construct a prima facie case, i.e., one that on its face presents a reasoned argument for the resolution. In order to structure a prima facie case, the affirmative must present the three general lines of value debate: definition, criteria, and justification. The strategies for initiating and supporting these lines of argument have been fully discussed in earlier chapters of this text. But remember, you must fulfill all of the prima facie requirements because there is no additional constructive speech to construct new arguments. The thorough discussion of the first affirmative constructive in team debate should acquaint you with the format for constructing the affirmative constructive in the Lincoln-Douglas format.

Negative Constructive

Like the affirmative constructive, the negative constructive constructs new arguments in the debate. As the only constructive speech that opposes the resolution, this speech establishes the arguments that form the negative attack. Unlike the affirmative constructive, the negative constructive can also concede and refute arguments in the debate. The negative constructive cannot extend arguments or repeat arguments since it has yet to present any arguments. If part of the affirmative constructive is blatantly true, the negative may choose not to waste time arguing the point. The negative may also have strategic reasons for conceding parts of the affirmative case. (Debaters should refer to Chapter Five of this text, "Interaction Among Lines of Argument," to help identify parts of the affirmative that are likely to create tensions with other arguments in the debate.) The negative constructive will want to refute the remaining claims of the affirmative constructive to prevent them from becoming winning arguments for the affirmative side.

If you return to the sample debate on televised trials, you will notice three negative responsibilities in the constructive speech: introduce the negative position; construct value objections; and refute affirmative arguments. The arguments must be thorough and complete. The negative also might refute any arguments that might win the debate for the affirmative debater. Failure to introduce a complete argument or respond to affirmative arguments can be troublesome because the negative has no other opportunity to make new arguments.

The negative constructive speaker should be alert to two very important distinctions in Lincoln-Douglas constructive presentations. First, there is less time to extend arguments in rebuttals. Thus, all positions need to be more fully developed. For the negative debater, this means that the negative position and countervalue objection need to very well structured. The value objection should certainly have the appropriate components of links, uniqueness, and impacts. In addition, the argument should include preemptions to likely affirmative responses. Wherever the negative argument is weakest, the affirmative is likely to attack. If you can anticipate an affirmative response, you may be well advised to answer the argument before it is given. One caveat: you can waste a lot of speech time preempting answers that are never made. You need to be careful to select preemptions carefully and make the arguments with a great deal of efficiency.

Second, there is no other opportunity to construct new arguments. Negative constructive speakers in Lincoln-Douglas debates need to be certain to answer all arguments in the affirmative constructive that might prove important. These arguments could include issues the affirmative will use to answer your arguments, or it could be arguments used to support the affirmative position. In this speech, the negative must address these important arguments or the debater will concede these arguments to the affirmative.

First Affirmative Rebuttal

The first affirmative rebuttal has four argument strategies available. In the first affirmative rebuttal, you can concede, refute, repeat, and extend arguments. In this speech you should respond to the negative position, answer the negative arguments through refutation and concession, and rebuild the affirmative case through extension. This is the only opportunity you have to respond before your last speech.

Failure to respond to any negative arguments now would concede the argument to the negative side. You should usually devote a good deal of time to answering any value objections, since losing a value objection could cost you the debate. Remember, even if your case is true, the negative can prove it is necessary to sacrifice the benefits of the resolution to avoid its disadvantages. You also need to be certain to extend all of the general lines of argument: topicality, criteria, and justification. Note any important arguments that the negative conceded to you and apply these arguments where you can to answer negative arguments. This will be more efficient than generating new answers. If your case is written strategically, you should be able to execute this strategy. Carefully read the second affirmative constructive and first affirmative rebuttal descriptions in the previous sections of this chapter to see how to execute the strategies of concession, refutation, repetition, and extension.

Negative Rebuttal

Like the affirmative rebuttalist, the negative rebuttalist can concede, repeat, refute, or extend arguments but not construct new arguments. The rebuttal speech summarizes why the negative should win the debate. The individual negative arguments should come together to deny the affirmative defense of the resolution.

Like the second negative rebuttalist in team debate, you should present the closing statements for the negative, extend the winning combination of arguments for the negative, and minimize winning affirmative arguments. Since this is the last opportunity to address the judge, you need to make the negative position extremely clear. You should prioritize arguments that can win the debate for the negative and select the strongest for extension early in your speech. You also need to minimize arguments that could win the round for the affirmative.

Some combination of maximizing the winning arguments of the negative and minimizing winning arguments from the affirmative must be accomplished first. After that, you can address additional arguments that may help win the debate. You may find it valuable to review the responsibilities of the second negative rebuttal speech in team debate for advice on how to perform this speech.

Second Affirmative Rebuttal

The second affirmative rebuttal is the mirror speech to the negative rebuttal. Like the previous two speeches, you can concede, repeat, refute, and extend arguments. The second affirmative rebuttal cannot initiate or construct new arguments. In the second affirmative rebuttal, you should present a strong summary of why the resolution is probably true.

The affirmative should present its closing statement, minimize the winning negative arguments, and maximize the winning affirmative arguments. This is the last speech the judge will hear in the debate. As a result, you must be certain to make the combination of winning arguments extremely clear. At the end of the speech, you must compare the resolutional values with the arguments proposed by the negative to provide the judge with a balanced perspective that enhances your position.

Remember that you need to win topicality, criteria, and justification to win the debate. Review the second affirmative rebuttal in the team debate section to understand how to implement these argumentative strategies.

Summary and Conclusions

In debate, several rules determine how the debates will proceed. Two sides, one affirmative and one negative, always debate according to a prescribed set of time limits and according to a designated speaking order. While some rules govern how arguments can be developed in these speeches, the debaters are generally free to argue their strongest case in whatever form they choose.

The requirements of the first affirmative constructive are that the speaker limit the speech to constructing arguments and that the three general lines of value argument occur either implicitly or explicitly. Debaters should word the first affirmative constructive powerfully and provide transitions that explain the logic of their case. In Lincoln-Douglas debate, the affirmative constructive must be especially thorough, since it is the speaker's only chance to construct arguments.

The first negative constructive must limit the development of arguments to construction, refutation, and concession. Traditionally, the first negative constructive introduces the negative position, and attacks the three general lines of value argument. In team debate, the first negative frequently introduces abbreviated versions of countervalue arguments and topicality arguments. In Lincoln-Douglas debate, the negative constructive must introduce more thoroughly developed countervalue arguments because there is only one constructive speech.

The second affirmative constructive can construct, concede, repeat, refute, or extend arguments in the debate. The second affirmative usually extends the affirmative case, refutes all attacks made in the first negative constructive, constructs additional justification for adopting the resolution, and preempts likely second negative attacks.

The second negative constructive can also construct, concede, repeat, refute, or extend arguments in the debate. Ordinarily, the second negative constructive extends the negative position, extends abbreviated versions of value objections, constructs new value objections or case attacks as needed, and refutes added justifications presented in the second affirmative constructive.

None of the rebuttal speeches in the debate can construct new arguments. The rebuttals resolve arguments through concession, repetition, refutation, and extension of previous arguments. Given the shorter time limits of the rebuttal speech, the rebuttalists must focus the debate to arguments that will win the debate for their side.

The first negative rebuttal extends attacks made against the general lines of argument, focuses the debate on issues that the negative is winning, aids the second negative constructive in coverage of any responses to major negative issues that remain unanswered, and extends any winning negative arguments not debated by the second negative constructive. The first affirmative rebuttal covers all the issues in the debate by refuting new arguments presented in the second negative constructive, extending the general lines of argument, and making selective responses to other negative arguments. The first affirmative rebuttal in Lincoln-Douglas debate similarly must answer all new arguments raised in the negative constructive, extend the general lines of argument, and make selective responses to other negative arguments.

The second negative rebuttal and the second affirmative rebuttal are the final speeches in the debate; these rebuttalists should summarize why their team is winning the debate. Ordinarily, these speakers open their rebuttal with a statement indicating the general reason they are winning, maximize the arguments that will help them win the debate, and minimize the winning arguments of the opposition. The negative rebuttal speaker and the second affirmative rebuttal speaker in

Lincoln-Douglas debate also summarize why the respective sides are winning the debate. They issue closing statements maximizing the arguments they are winning and minimizing the winning arguments of their opponent.

In this chapter we summarized the conventions regarding placement of particular issues in the debate. Previous chapters in the core text and this volume outline how to accomplish these objectives. Knowledge of the conventional placement of arguments is important because it generally has strategic value for debaters. If, however, you discover that alternative placement of the issues is more beneficial, feel free to break from conventional placement. Debaters should remember that judges expect debate strategies to be fair to both sides in the debate and educational to all participants in the debate. You should be certain that unconventional approaches to the duties of the speakers are consistent with the principles of competitive fairness and academic integrity.

Exercises

1. Imagine that you are debating against a case that argues that nude dancing should be a protected form of free speech. You plan to argue that such expression has no value and is, in fact, objectionable because it degrades women. Write a negative position statement that encompasses all of your arguments.

2. Find three of your classmates and participate in a debate. Designate one person the first affirmative, one the second affirmative, one the first negative, and one the second negative. Pick a topic you will all enjoy debating, then incorporate all of the speaker roles specified in this chapter. Use time limits of 8 minutes for constructives and 5 minutes for rebuttals. If you prefer Lincoln-Douglas, pick one classmate and perform the exercise using the Lincoln-Douglas format suggested in the chapter.

3. Find a debate on C-SPAN or public television. Watch until you can identify examples of each of the following techniques: construction, concession, refutation, repetition, extension. Make sure your examples are consistent with the definitions of these terms provided in this chapter.

7

Evaluating the Debate

Chapter Outline

Audience Analysis
Paradigms
    Hypothesis-Testing
    Philosophical Systems
    Critic of Argument
    Tabula Rasa
    Games Theorists
    Skills Assessment
Determining the Judge's Perspective
    Previous Ballots
    Networking
    Publications
    Nonverbal Feedback
Determining Your Own Perspective
Summary and Conclusions

Key Terms

audience analysis
paradigms
hypothesis-testers
philosophical systems
critics of argument
tabula rasa
games theorists
skills assessment

The judges of a debate have no easy task to perform. They must be, of course, unprejudiced as to the subject. They must not forget that they are to decide on the merits of the debate, not on the merits of the question. . . . They must neither be stupefied by dull figures which may yet be pertinent, nor, on the other hand, be hypnotized by brilliant rhetoric which may be but effervescent after all. They must sift, analyze, weigh, decide. It is a task but little easier than that of the debaters themselves.

William Horton Foster
Debating for Boys, 1922

In the preceding chapters we have identified the lines of argument generally available for affirming and negating a value-debate resolution. You should not conclude from these chapters that it is easy for judges to determine which side wins or loses these arguments or how these arguments interrelate. You have a responsibility as a debater to persuade the judge that your arguments are sufficient to win the debate.

Judges try to be impartial, assessing each debate as fairly and conscientiously as possible. However, evaluating a debate is not simple. The complexity of arguments in any one debate can be staggering, impressing the judge with well-reasoned positions on both affirmative and negative sides of the resolution. In close debates, judges frequently resort to their own attitudes and beliefs in resolving difficult disputes.

Audience Analysis

In order to enhance the persuasiveness of your arguments, you should become familiar with some fundamental tenets of audience analysis. **Audience analysis** is the attempt by speakers to identify the beliefs, values, and attitudes of their audiences. Audience analysis is a highly imperfect discipline. However, anytime you attempt to persuade another individual or group, audience analysis is vital in order to be effective. Lobbyists before Congress, who frequently recommend that Congress uphold the very values you are proposing in debates, engage in systematic audience analysis. They identify the voting records of important legislators, determine the legislators' place on the political spectrum from conservative to liberal, and understand the voting constituency to which a legislator must respond to determine if personal and political interest will sway a vote in their direction. At that point, lobbyists tailor their messages to appeal to the beliefs and attitudes of those congressional actors they assess as most important to a successful lobbying campaign. Similarly, candidates for public office, attorneys before juries and judges, advertising executives, and entertainers all engage in sophisticated analyses of their audience in order to mount the most appealing messages they can identify.

While debate is an academic exercise that judges would like to evaluate with an open mind, that standard is nearly impossible to achieve. The closer the debate, the more difficulty judges will have not falling back on their own biases. Debaters need to adapt their messages to be consistent with the attitudes and beliefs of their judges. Many areas of bias can enter into a judge's decision making, but we believe three areas tend to surface more than others. Judges can have strong political beliefs, strong beliefs about the purposes of debate, and strong beliefs about the role of the judge in a debate.

Debate judges certainly attempt to leave their political and social biases at the door. However, when a debate is close these sociopolitical beliefs might determine how they resolve nearly equal issues. Judges might find evidence from sources who are consistent with their own beliefs more credible than evidence from sources with whom they disagree. They might find the reasoning of those who agree with their own political beliefs more persuasive. If you take positions that are directly opposed to the political beliefs of your judge, you may find it difficult to win a close debate. If you must take a position inconsistent with his or her sociopolitical beliefs, you should attempt to present that position in the most positive light. You should not take positions that directly oppose the judge's worldview. Instead, you should attempt to find areas of agreement between the position you are taking in the debate and the beliefs and attitudes of your critic.

Many judges also have beliefs and attitudes about the role debate should play in the life of the debater. As a result, they may carry assumptions into the debate round that can directly influence how they decide some arguments. Some judges believe that debate should teach students the persuasive skills of a good public speaker. These individuals might pay less attention to the exact wording of opposing evidence. Instead, they might place more emphasis on persuasive presentation. Other judges believe that debate should teach students the process of argumentation and support with little regard for the skills of public presentation. Such individuals will devote more of their decision making to considering who presents the more compelling reasoning and evidence rather than who presented the reasoning and evidence in the more persuasive fashion.

> Obviously the manner of the speaker has a more immediate appeal than the subject matter. However, a debate is not a declamation contest. It is a presentation of arguments for or against a proposition so arranged and related that they move to an irresistable conclusion. Certainly what the debater says is more important that how he says it. It would be impossible to define the relative importance of the two divisions of the subject.
>
> William Horton Foster
> *Debating for Boys*, 1922

Sometimes you will find yourself debating before judges who have little exposure to competitive academic debates. These individuals could include school administrators or interested members of the community who have been asked to evaluate your debates. These judges may have little academic training in debate, but you should respect their perspective and expectations. You should certainly not assume that they are unable to evaluate the debate with expertise. In fact, studies indicate that these critics are likely to vote in accordance with the decisions rendered by more experienced debate judges. The previous chapters of this book and the core text emphasize that the general lines of argument in debate are appropriate for value debating in any format. As a debater, you should be able to communicate to the most inexperienced judge the definition of terms, the criteria for evaluating values, and the justification for values affirmed in the resolution. When challenging the four general lines of argument, you should be able to communicate the failure of the affirmative to fulfill these arguments and why the failure to fulfill these arguments justifies negating the resolution. Remember, judges are not required to adapt to you; you must adapt to your judges.

Paradigms

Judges have personal and professional biases toward the issues in the debate as well as toward the purposes of debate. Many of these individuals also have systematic frameworks for assessing entire debates. You can best understand these frameworks, called **paradigms,** as analogies that judges draw between debate and some other social activities that require evaluation. One critic, for example, might consider debate to most closely resemble a criminal courtroom, complete with a prosecutor (the affirmative side, which is responsible for making a case for the resolution), a defense attorney (the negative side, which makes a case denying the resolution), and a judge. Following this analogy, these critics would require proof beyond reasonable doubt prior to their affirmation of the resolution.

The judge's use of a paradigm in the evaluation of a debate has many advantages. First, the paradigm helps the judge determine the strength of each argument within a debate. As an example, the critic might want to know how significantly the affirmative team would have to justify the resolution to convincingly argue that the resolution should be affirmed. In the criminal courtroom analogy, the requirement is proof beyond a reasonable doubt. Using other paradigms, the judge might be satisfied with, for example, only a preponderance of the evidence standard. Paradigms, then, give guidance about how to evaluate each argument in a debate.

Second, the paradigm is likely to produce more consistent evaluation from one debate round to the next. Letting an analogy guide the selection of important arguments within a debate makes it easier for judges to avoid voting for debate teams merely because they like them better than their opponents. The paradigm helps provide objectivity from debate to debate. The guidelines remain consistent, so the evaluation of arguments takes on a similar consistency.

Finally, a paradigm provides debaters with some forewarning about how a judge will assess a debate. Because the paradigm indicates how the judge will likely evaluate particular arguments, the debater can anticipate how a given judge is likely to respond. The debaters can envision themselves in a role consistent with the analogy that the judge is using, gaining insight into the strength and relevance of their claims.

Despite these advantages, paradigms have their drawbacks. On some occasions, judges will appear to accept a paradigm but ignore the implications of that paradigm for certain arguments. This situation occurs because the debater may misinterpret the paradigm that the judge is using or the judge may not fully understand or accept the full set of guidelines for a particular paradigm. Given the imprecise application of these approaches, debaters should be prepared to make arguments that are persuasive across paradigms or to make claims that persuade the judge that a single argument fits into his or her specific paradigm.

In some instances, judges and debaters are completely conscious of the paradigm guiding their evaluation and the argumentative implications of that paradigm. Nevertheless, the paradigm can never offer a perfect representation of a debate round. A courtroom trial, after all, is not an academic debate as defined in this textbook. Differences emerge between the debate and the processes in the analogy. When these differences arise, debaters cannot anticipate how the judge will resolve the issue based on an understanding of the paradigm alone. The judges themselves may be forced to rely on their intuition to make the determination. Debaters must instead argue actively and carefully for a favorable decision under the terms of the paradigm as they understand it.

This textbook provides debaters with an approach that allows them to minimize the pitfalls of judges' paradigms. The primary reason is that the general lines of argument for value debate are applicable in all paradigms. If debaters can master the general lines of argument, they can develop an arsenal of arguments that allow them the flexibility to succeed regardless of a judge's preference of paradigm. While knowledge of the implications of paradigms will not guarantee the debater success, such information will be helpful in determining the perspective of the evaluator.

To maximize the strategic opportunities in this argumentative arsenal, debaters must understand the paradigms and their implications for arguments. In the remainder of this chapter we outline the predominant paradigms, emphasizing their assumptions and implications for the general lines of argument for value debate. Paradigms, unlike sociopolitical biases and educational perspectives, have a direct relationship with the lines of argument we have been discussing. We, therefore, discuss the relationship between paradigms and the general lines of argument in some detail.

Our list of paradigms is not exhaustive. We have tried to focus on those paradigms that many judges find useful when evaluating debates. Many others exist today, and even more paradigms will emerge in the future. Debate theory is constantly evolving. Debaters should be prepared to adapt to changes generally accepted by most of the debate community or by their individual judges.

Hypothesis-Testing

Hypothesis-testers view themselves as scientific theorists. Like the scientist, the hypothesis-tester attempts to test the probable truth or falsity of a claim. In debate, this claim is the resolution, with the hypothesis-tester seeking to understand if the claim in its entirety is a "probably true" statement.

Presumption for the hypothesis-tester always rests against the resolution. The reason lies in the analogy to science. When scientists seek to understand some relationship, they use the *null hypothesis*. The null hypothesis assumes that no relationship exists. As an example, a scientist attempting to discover whether saccharin causes cancer would test the null hypothesis that saccharin does not cause cancer. By testing the relationship in this manner, scientists can rule out alternative causes that might result in cancer. In a debate, the hypothesis-tester works according to the same logic. By assuming that the resolution is false, the hypothesis-tester always grants presumption to the negative team.

In order to uphold the burden of proving the probable truth of the resolution, the affirmative must define the terms much like scientists must define the parameters of their study. The negative can argue that the hypothesis (the resolution) is probably false by proving that the affirmative has incorrectly defined the terms in the hypothesis. Since the affirmative has the burden of proving the resolution is probably true, the affirmative must meet the parameters of the debate topic. Many hypothesis-testers in value debate believe that when the affirmative inadequately defines terms, they may be susceptible to the hasty generalization or whole-resolution argument. The negative has only to argue that the affirmative has failed to prove the probable truth of the resolution. If the affirmative example is not representative of the resolution or if the resolution might be untrue for reasons the affirmative ignores, the negative may convince the hypothesis-tester that the resolution is probably false.

The affirmative must establish criteria for determining the probable truth of the resolution. The hypothesis-tester needs a method of determining whether the hypothesis is probably true or probably false. If the negative can prove that the affirmative's criteria are completely inadequate, the judge cannot evaluate the probable truth of the hypothesis. Of course, the negative can present countercriteria, but for the hypothesis-tester, countercriteria are probably not necessary. If the affirmative fails to provide an adequate basis for determining the validity of the hypothesis, then the hypothesis-tester cannot assess the probable truth of the resolution and will vote negative.

The affirmative justification is necessary to complete the proof of the hypothesis. Just as the scientist must conduct an experiment to prove the hypothesis is true, the debater uses the justification of the value as a way to conduct the experiment. The judge uses the justification argument to test the validity of the resolution. If the justification proves that the resolution is probably true according to the criteria, then the hypothesis-tester is likely to affirm the resolution.

The negative can attack the justification as an inadequate proof of the resolution. The negative can offer countervalue objections to prove the value trades off with more important values. Some hypothesis-testers believe that the negative can argue that more representative examples of the resolution can prove that the resolution is not justified. If the affirmative offers a narrow test of the resolution, but the negative offers a more representative example of the resolution, then the judge may decide that the resolution is generally false.

Philosophical Systems

The **philosophical systems** paradigm focuses much more on the criteria for comparing the values defended by the affirmative and the negative. The philosophical systems approach, therefore, interfaces somewhat differently with the general lines of argument than the hypothesis-testing paradigm does.

The fundamental difference between the hypothesis-tester and the philosophical systems judge is on the focus of the debate. The hypothesis-tester asks, "Is the resolution probably true or probably false?" The philosophical systems judge asks, "Which ethical system should I prefer: the affirmative's or the negative's?" As a result of the differing perspective, these judges frequently view debates differently. Hypothesis-testers focus on the resolution as a whole. Philosophical systems judges focus on the comparison of two systems. Presumption is always against the resolution for the hypothesis-tester. For the philosophical systems judge, presumption can sometimes rest with the affirmative if the criteria justify that argument.

The philosophical systems approach recognizes that the affirmative must meet the parameters of the resolution. The resolution sets the ground for comparing values. However, unlike many hypothesis-testers, the philosophical systems judge finds hasty generalization and whole-resolution arguments less persuasive. The philosophical systems judge wants to compare the philosophical issues of the affirmative with the philosophical issues of the negative. The truth of the resolution as a whole is not an issue for most philosophical systems judges.

The philosophical systems approach places a great deal of emphasis on the criteria used in the debate. Philosophical systems judges prefer a criterion that stems from the resolution and is consistent with other established philosophical arguments. In value debates, the philosophical systems of such writers as John Stuart Mill, John Rawls, and Richard Dworkin provide analogous criteria for debaters. Negative debaters usually need to either meet the affirmative criteria or defend superior countercriteria. In arguing that the affirmative criteria are inadequate, the negative will probably have to offer an alternative system. Most of these judges will settle for weak affirmative criteria rather than vote against the resolution. The negative needs to defend countercriteria to maximize its chances with this judge.

The philosophical systems judge views the justification as important to determining the impact of supporting certain value systems. If the negative can indicate that more important issues are compromised by the affirmative's values, then the judge needs to negate the resolution. However, the philosophical systems judge is less likely to listen to value objections that apply generally to the resolution. Objections linked to the philosophical positions or criteria of the affirmative tend to be more persuasive.

For the philosophical systems judge, presumption can vary with the resolution and the criteria defended by the affirmative. If the affirmative is defending a resolution that affirms individual rights, there are some philosophical systems that indicate that some rights *always* deserve presumption. If the affirmative is defending a resolution that increases social welfare programs, there are some philosophical systems that indicate that human welfare *always* deserve presumption. The resolution and the criteria determine who has presumption in the debate.

The remaining paradigms in debate lack the level of development that hypothesis-testing and philosophical system models offer. Rather than provide guidance concerning each of the three general lines of argument, they work from a basic assumption that determines how the judge should evaluate each argument in a debate. While we will treat each of these four paradigms individually in this chapter, debaters should be aware that many judges use assumptions of these paradigms in conjunction with other basic assumptions about how to evaluate debates.

Critic of Argument

> The other possibility . . . is a critic's vote, or expert's vote, giving expert opinion as to the comparative excellence of the debating done.
>
> O'Neill, Laycock, and Scales
> *Argumentation and Debate,* 1920

Judges who consider themselves to be **critics of argument** assume that the debaters must master a certain quality of argument to be persuasive. The standards for what constitutes a good argument vary from judge to judge, but they generally require analytical reasoning, evidentiary support, and assessments of the argument's impact within the context of the whole debate. If a debater fails to provide evidence or reasoning to bolster a given claim, the critic of argument will likely ignore the issue altogether. Weak arguments, even if the opposing team does not refute them, are seldom voting issues in the context of the debate. Critics of argument try to avoid bringing their predispositions about particular types of debate arguments (e.g., presumption, the function of criteria, hasty generalization) into the debate. Instead, they rely on the strength of the debaters' evidence and reasoning to assess all lines of argument.

Tabula Rasa

In many ways, the **tabula rasa** judge is the antithesis of the critic of argument. This judging philosophy views the judge's mind as a "blank slate" that debaters "write on" when they debate. The judge is to minimize the use of personal preferences or arbitrary requirements for evaluating a debate. Complete open-mindedness is the goal of judges using this paradigm. As a result, the judge places a premium on the debaters' ability to evaluate and summarize the issues within a debate. Arguments that opposing teams fail to refute become voting issues. Standards for what constitutes a good argument are left to the debaters to argue in the debate. Basic expectations or argumentative burdens discussed throughout this book are always open to debate for the tabula rasa judge. If affirmative debaters argue that they should not have to provide criteria for evaluating competing values and the negative team cannot articulate why the affirmative should have to demonstrate criteria, this general line of argument would not enter into the judge's evaluation.

Some modified tabula rasa judges recognize that taking this philosophy to its extreme could lead to absurd evaluations of debates. If one team insists that each team must tell a joke every twenty seconds of their speaking time to win and the opposing team fails to explain why this standard should not exist, should the first team win the debate, regardless of the worth of the rest of its arguments? The modified tabula rasa judge intervenes into the debate only long enough to reject a blatantly silly argument, whether it is refuted or not. All other arguments, however, remain for the debaters to resolve in the context of the debate.

Games Theorists

> The custom has grown in recent years of referring to contest debate as a sport or game . . . this conception helps us to decide on proper grounds, and frees us from much cant and hypocrisy.
>
> O'Neill, Laycock, and Scales
> *Argumentation and Debate,* 1920.

Games theorists do not view debate as a test of a hypothesis or as a clash of philosophical systems. Rather, they view debate as a competitive contest in which each side must have an equal opportunity to win. The governing standard for evaluating any argument in this paradigm is fairness. While the notion of fairness varies from one debate judge to another, all games theorists expect the debaters to explain any stances on the theoretical issues of the debate as they effect the competitive fairness of debate. Theoretical issues in a debate are the "rules" by which the debaters play the game. Who gets the right to define the terms of the resolution? Does a countervalue have to be unique? What standard of evidence is appropriate for establishing the case for affirming a particular value? Debaters must resolve these issues and others like them in such a way that each team retains an equal opportunity to win. Arguments indicating that one team receives a competitive advantage as a result of a particular theoretical issue have a strong persuasive effect on the games theorist.

Some debate judges view games theory as the umbrella paradigm that encompasses all other paradigms and their attendant rules. These judges feel that the issue of fairness is of such paramount importance that issues of how a philosopher would act or how a scientist might proceed are secondary. Regardless of which role the judge assumes, these individuals consider fairness to be a prior concern.

Skills Assessment

Some judges evaluate the debates according to a skills assessment perspective. Rather than placing exclusive emphasis on argument and evidence, the **skills assessment** perspective expects debaters to demonstrate communication and argumentation *skills.* These judges look for debaters to demonstrate many of the skills necessary for persuasive public presentation. They want debaters to demonstrate the qualities you expect in any public speaker: forceful delivery, powerful language, vocal inflection, and good character are all important factors in deciding who won or lost the debate. While argument construction, supporting evidence, and refutation of opponent's arguments are important, the skills assessment judge considers how the public audience would perceive the arguments, evidence, and refutation. The debater who incorporates the fundamental skills of public presentation with quality analysis will be the most successful debater in front of any judge. But the qualities of public speaking are more important before the skills assessment judge.

Determining the Judge's Perspective

This chapter has assumed that you can identify what influences a judge's perspective. In many instances, however, you may not know the judge well enough to know his or her sociopolitical beliefs, attitudes toward debate students, or beliefs about a judge's role in debate. Since debaters' success can frequently turn on their ability to understand the framework within which the judge is either implicitly or explicitly operating, the remainder of the chapter offers some suggestions for identifying a judge's biases.

Though these recommendations apply most directly to tournament debating, you can use many of the same principles in your classroom. Remember that the instructor who judges you must be treated like a person, not an evaluation machine. By talking with fellow students, members of past classes and, of course, the instructor, you can get a much better idea of how to frame your arguments for greatest effect.

Previous Ballots

Debaters have an important opportunity to understand their judges by carefully considering the written comments of that judge in previous rounds. The ballot may reveal that the judge finds some sources of evidence or arguments with a liberal or conservative twist more persuasive than others. The ballot may expose the judge's view of the function of debate in the student's education by the comments on style and presentation. The ballot may indicate that the judge finds a certain countervalue too generic to be persuasive, that the debaters failed to provide sufficient reasoning to sustain their arguments, or that the judge considers whole-resolution arguments an ineffective strategy. Comments like these, coupled with an understanding of the assumptions of the paradigms outlined in this chapter, allow the debater to predict how that same judge is likely to evaluate other issues in future debates.

Networking

Debaters should speak with former colleagues, former and current debaters, and current debate coaches from the judge's region of the country to discover a judge's perspective. Just because one debater does not know a given individual does not mean that other debaters would not be invaluable sources of information.

Publications

Many debate judges publish articles and books outlining how debates should be evaluated. *Argumentation and Advocacy,* formerly the *Journal of the American Forensic Association, Speaker and Gavel, Rostrum* and the *C.E.D.A. Yearbook* are national publications that contain important articles on debate evaluation. Argumentation conferences, such as the Alta Conference, publish proceedings that record many individual judging philosophies. Debate handbooks may contain articles by prominent debate judges, and debate textbooks may offer other insight. By keeping up-to-date on what members of the debate community are publishing, debaters will gain insight into the argumentative preferences of their judges.

Nonverbal Feedback

Frequently, despite your best efforts, you will be unable to find out anything about your judge before a round begins. That does not mean, however, that you have exhausted your options for learning about your judge's probable reactions. During an actual debate, debaters will often receive nonverbal responses concerning the quality of their arguments. The judge may nod along with winning arguments, frown during arguments that are less appealing, or even wave debaters past uninteresting issues. If debaters are careful to process this feedback, not as a personal insult, but as a comment on the types of arguments they are initiating, they may be able to glean the judge's perspective.

We must conclude this discussion with a word of warning. While it is important to use a variety of cues to determine your judge's preferences, you should not depend too much on these forms of feedback. Debate judges cannot be stereotyped any more than any other individuals. The differences between your expectations and a judge's actual preferences can sometimes be shocking, and failure to respect individuals because you categorize their beliefs based on appearance or background can also be terribly insulting. Polling surveys, for example, indicate that in elections, African-Americans vote a liberal ticket approximately ninety percent of the time. However, you would be foolish to assume that all African-Americans are political liberals. Many prominent African-Americans scoff at the notion of liberal politics. Supreme Court Justice Clarence Thomas is just one example of a prominent, conservative African-American. Many Jewish voters tend to support pro-Israel congressional and senatorial candidates. However, many American Jewish voters would also rather see Israel seek accommodation with the Palestinians and Israel's neighboring Arab states and condemn "hard-line" confrontational policies. Stereotyping can lead you to false conclusions as well as to offensive behavior.

Further, when you use generalized criteria (such as a paradigm) to better understand your judge, you do not want to sound as if you are pandering to his or her personal biases. By overemphasizing expected biases, you risk insulting and alienating judges who do not like to be categorized. You should always respect the cognitive ability of your audience, which includes an acknowledgement that people come to different conclusions in different situations. If you assume that judges are unable to listen to all sides of an issue because that issue conflicts with their sociopolitical beliefs, their views of what debate should mean for the student who participates, or their normal judging paradigm, you will likely insult your judge. Recognize that judges strive toward intellectual honesty; they also strive to allow debaters to control the arguments in debate regardless of the judge's personal beliefs.

> . . . at least occasionally visit with them, always be cognizant of their proceedings and let their reports be given to you for this purpose. Thus, you will have provided for them a most profitable as well as most exciting exercise. Young men will find that its invitations are stronger than the saloon and the frivolous society, and all will, in after life, cherish it as their most valuable school-work. It may cost you an effort, it may task your ingenuity, it may sometimes weary your patience; but what attainments do we have that do not require our best injuries? Surely none.
>
> O. P. Kinsley
> *The Normal Debater*, 1876

Determining Your Own Perspective

Up to this point, this chapter has described the debate evaluation process in terms of the judge exclusively. While this approach may make you more persuasive or potentially more successful in your debates, it is still a narrow view of the debate process. You can also use the basic principles of debate evaluation to determine your own perspective about your participation in the activity.

Ask yourself, what am I doing when I debate? Am I learning to test the truth of arguments? Am I learning important speech skills? Am I learning to evaluate public arguments? Am I playing games? Your purposes for engaging in value debate should guide your approach to it. Debate is an educational activity in which you can establish your personal objectives. Explore and establish your own goals and objectives. Seek the advice of instructors to help determine the viability of those objectives and the best avenues for achieving them.

The different paradigms for viewing debate can help you determine what is important and what is unimportant in the activity. Being aware of your perspective allows you to identify modern conventions of debate that do not further your own goals. It also permits you to focus your energies on the debate process. By exploring differing perspectives on the dynamic activity of debate, you can understand how debate functions as a competitive and educational activity.

By exploring different perspectives on debate, you can better understand other activities. The perspectives we discuss on debate are borrowed from other fields of study: science, communication, philosophy, and other academic disciplines. You can take these analogs a step further and find them in other parts of your life. By comparing the processes and interrelationships between fields, you can expand your perspective on many interests in your life.

> To be a poor debater at first is not proof that you cannot ultimately succeed.
> Some of the most celebrated debaters of history were woefully weak in oratory,
> but attained well-deserved eminence by persevering, against all discouragements,
> in their determinations to conquer every obstacle.
>
> A. H. Craig
> *Pros and Cons*, 1897

You might also find that exploring perspectives will lead you to change the way you view debate. Different perspectives might capture your attention or interests at different times. This is also a healthy practice. Changing times alter what we think. When you sense a change of perspective, it will be helpful to ask yourself why you are leaning toward a different perspective and what the purpose of this new perspective is. As we grow and find new ways of looking at things, it helps to compare our new perspective to where we have been. What made the change happen and why are you tempted or compelled by it? The views we discover in debate can have a great influence on our worldviews. We should approach them with the same spirit of critical inquiry we bring to debate.

Throughout this book, you have been asked to examine the process of debate through a lines of argument perspective. The place to begin your critical assessment is here. If you discover that the lines of argument approach is useful for you, begin to ask why. Would the approach be applicable to other aspects of your life? What are the strengths and weaknesses of the perspective? What do you gain? What is left to explore?

Summary and Conclusions

Despite strong efforts to remain impartial, judges must rely on their personal frameworks for assessing the complexity of many debates. These frameworks may include judges' sociopolitical beliefs, their interpretation of the purpose of debate, and their interpretations of the role of the debate judge. The frameworks that describe the role of the judge are called paradigms. Paradigms are analogies drawn between debate and other aspects of society that involve some sort of evaluation. All judges implicitly or explicitly adhere to some paradigm.

Paradigms have both advantages and disadvantages. On the positive side, a paradigm can provide guidance to the judge for determining the relative merit of particular arguments in the debate, can offer a consistent method of debate evaluation, and can help debaters predict how a judge will view a particular argument. The drawbacks of paradigms include their inconsistent or overly rigid application by judges and their inability to explain all aspects of debate.

Hypothesis-testers consider their role as debate evaluator to be like that of a scientist researching a claim of probable truth. Presumption is always against the resolution. Affirmative teams must define terms clearly in order to determine if the resolution is probably true. Hasty generalization and whole-resolution arguments can be compelling to the hypothesis-tester. If the affirmative debaters cannot defend their criteria as appropriate, they will probably lose the debate. Without criteria to evaluate the justification argument, the resolution cannot be tested. Countervalues that link to the resolution as a whole are sometimes acceptable to hypothesis-testers.

Philosophical systems judges view their role as a philosopher choosing between competing value systems. Presumption can vary depending on the criteria or the resolution. While topicality is important, this judge does not consider hasty generalization or whole-resolution arguments valid objections. The philosophical systems judge also finds criteria important, but the negative must establish a countercriteria or meet the affirmative criteria to win the debate. Countervalue objections that link to the resolution as a whole, instead of the criteria or justification defended by the affirmative, are usually not persuasive to this judge. The philosophical systems judge seeks to compare ethical systems for choosing between competing values.

The critic of argument establishes standards for "good" argument, usually stressing the need for analytical reasoning, evidentiary support, and understanding of impact in relation to the other arguments in the debate. Tabula rasa judges assume that the debate judge should be completely impartial, bringing no predetermined standards to bear on a debate. The games theorist treats debate as a competitive contest in which both teams should have an equal opportunity to win. The skills assessment judge views the debate from the perspective of a public audience and expects debaters to demonstrate strong public presentation skills.

To determine the paradigm that is either implicitly or explicitly guiding a particular judge's evaluation procedure, debaters have several options. They can carefully assess judges' written comments on previous ballots, they can network with colleagues and debaters familiar with a given judge, they can keep abreast of debate publications that indicate the preferences of some debate judges, and they can react to the nonverbal feedback that occurs in a debate.

While understanding the evaluation process of the judge is useful, debaters should also examine evaluation from a personal perspective. The various analogs discussed in this chapter can help debaters ask, what am I doing when I debate? The answers to this most important question can provide debaters with a means of judging their participation not only in debate, but in other life activities as well.

Exercises

1. Assume you are watching a debate in which one team is clearly the stronger of the two. The better team has superior speaking skills, has superior evidence, and wins every argument in the debate—except one. The team does not respond to an asserted argument that the strength of the value objections outweighs the case justification. Who wins the debate? Evaluate the debate from the perspectives of each of the paradigms discussed in this chapter.

2. Imagine that you are watching a debate where the affirmative debaters defines their terms implicitly. The negative argues that the affirmative should lose the debate because their definitions are not explicit. The negative reasons that we cannot debate whether or not something is true if we do not know what it is. The affirmative responds that they should be able to define terms implicitly. The justification and criteria arguments let the negative know the subject of the debate. Who wins the debate? Would the different paradigms resolve the debate differently?

3. Suppose that you are debating against an affirmative that supports the resolution, "Resolved: that fetal rights deserve more protection in the United States." The judge assigned to your debate has a reputation for being a strong pro-life advocate. How can you convince the judge to vote against the affirmative? What arguments might be persuasive? How could you phrase the arguments so they would not alienate the judge? How would your arguments change if your judge were pro-choice?

Glossary

A

add-on additional reasoning explaining why the judge should affirm the resolution. Add-ons appear in the second affirmative constructive speech.

affirmative the side in the debate charged with defending the debate resolution.

audience analysis the attempt by a speaker to identify the beliefs, values, and attitudes of an audience.

B

better definition a topicality standard that indicates that the better definition read in the debate should be used to interpret the resolution.

brief an essentially complete argument or chain of reasoning that you expect to use in a debate.

brink the point at which the impact of an argument becomes inevitable.

burden of proof (1) the requirement that sufficient evidence or reasoning to prove an argument be presented. (2) when applied to the affirmative, the requirement that those affirming a value resolution must demonstrate topicality, criteria, and justification.

C

case argumentation representing the rationale for the resolution, referring to both affirmative and negative arguments over topicality, criteria, and justification. Also called affirmative case.

citation specific information on the source of evidence including publication, date of publication, page excerpt, and author's qualifications.

complementary argument an argument that supports the reasoning of another claim in a debate.

concession granting an argument to an opponent, either by direct reference or by failure to answer opposing arguments.

conditional argument an argument that depends on a set of specified circumstances. Such an argument can be conceded without detrimental effect on a side's other arguments in the debate.

construction the initiation of new claims into a debate.

constructive speeches in which the debaters are allowed to initiate new arguments.

contention (1) a major point advanced in the debate. (2) a subdivision of an affirmative case.

context (1) a standard for evaluating topicality arguments to determine if the definitions offered in the debate are consistent with the meaning of other words in the resolution. (2) the relationship of the evidence read in the debate to the original source material.

contradictory argument an argument that disproves the assumptions or claims made previously by the same side in a debate.

countervalue objection an argument that indicates that competing values are more important than the value affirmed in the resolution. Also called countervalue or value objection.

countervalues an argument that indicates that competing values are more important than the value affirmed in the resolution. Also called countervalue objection or value objection.

criteria *type of argument that establishes a method for evaluating the probable truth of a value resolution.*

critic of argument *an evaluator who believes the debaters must master a certain quality of argument to be persuasive.*

cross-application *when an argument is applied to more than one position.*

cross-examination *a specified period of time reserved in the debate for each side to ask questions of the other speaker, usually between the constructive speeches.*

D

debatability *a topicality standard that argues that as long as a definition provides fair grounds for debate, it should be accepted.*

degree of reparability *a standard for assessing the impact of an argument based on projections of the degree to which society can recover from the effects.*

disadvantages *a deleterious or undesirable consequence of affirming the resolution (sometimes referred to as "D.A." or "Disad."). See also value objection or countervalue objection.*

dropping an argument *failure to respond to an opponent's argument.*

E

evidence *quotations that tend to prove or provide grounds for arguments.*

extension *a line of argument that elaborates on the original point by either directly clashing with the argument against the original point or by expanding the scope of the original argument.*

F

flowcharting *note-taking in debates.*

G

game theorist *an evaluator who views debate as a competitive contest in which each side must have an equal chance to win.*

grammatical context *the topicality standard that holds that the grammatical function of a word within a sentence should help govern the word's meaning*

grouping arguments *identification of similar arguments that can be answered by discovering their common weakness.*

H

hasty generalization *(1) in nonpolicy debate, an argument that suggests that the affirmative justification is not sufficiently representative to imply the probable truth of the resolution. (2) a common fallacy of argument in which the speaker implies a general truth from a specific example.*

hypothesis-testers *an evaluator who views the judge's role as testing the probable truth or falsity of a claim.*

I

impact *(1) the consequences of an argument in a debate. (2) the good or bad results of affirming or negating the resolution.*

implicit definition *when debaters present their criteria and their justification as an operational definition of the resolution.*

independent arguments *a claim that relies on no other claim in the debate to serve as a reason to affirm or negate the resolution.*

irrelevancy *an argument that has no bearing on the issue at hand.*

J

judge *the person who evaluates the debate and is empowered to declare a winner.*

justification *arguments that illustrate the practical significance of a value argument.*

L

linear argument *a line of argument that establishes that for every incremental increase in cause there is an inevitable increase in effect.*

link *(1) the part of the argument that establishes a connection between a premise and a conclusion. (2) to create the relationship that illustrates that affirming one value means the judge rejects a competing countervalue.*

M

magnitude *a line of argument supporting justification that deals with the degree of importance that individuals attach to the value.*

moral imperative *an argument that suggests that members of society have some ethical responsibilities that are fundamental to human order.*

N

negative *the side in the debate charged with denying the resolution.*

negative position statement
statement that overviews and
encompasses all the negative
arguments in a debate and
establishes an argumentative
tie between them.

O

off-case a reference that
identifies values that
compete with the values
specified in the resolution.

P

paradigm an analogy that a
judge draws between debate
and other activities that
require evaluation.

philosophical systems a
judging paradigm focusing
on the criteria for comparing
the values defended by the
affirmative and the negative.

presumption (1) the
assumption that the
resolution is false until
shown to be otherwise. (2)
The assumed importance of
fundamental values.

prima facie case a series of
arguments presented by the
affirmative that, on its face,
presents a reasoned
argument for the resolution.

probability the likelihood that
something is true. In causal
reasoning this would include
the likelihood that one thing
will cause another. In
prediction this would
include the likelihood that
something is going to occur.

Q

quasi-policy resolutions
value-debate resolutions that
identify a government action
as a method of affirming an
explicit or implicit value.

R

reasonability a topicality
standard that requires the
affirmative to offer a
definition that is not overly
broad.

rebuttal a speech in which the
debaters resolve competing
claims that have already
been initiated.

refutation the process of
denying the reasoning of an
opponent's arguments.

repetition the repeating of an
argument for emphasis.

resolution the central issue
under discussion that the
affirmative must defend and
the negative must deny.

S

scope a line of argument
supporting justification that
identifies the number of
people to whom the value
has importance.

skills assessment a judging
philosophy that views the
debater's ability to
demonstrate communication
and argumentation skills as
the paramount concern.

social significance a line of
argument supporting
justification holding that
some values are justified
because they are beneficial to
society as a whole.

specificity of impact a
standard for assessing the
impact of an argument
involving the degree of detail
provided for the
argumentative scenario.

T

tabula rasa a judging
philosophy that views the
judge's mind as a blank
slate that debaters write on
when they debate.

threshold the point at which
the impact of an argument
becomes inevitable.

time frame a measure of how
long it will take for
something to occur.

topical the quality of
fulfilling the requirements of
the resolution.

topicality the line of
argument about whether or
not the affirmative case falls
within the scope of the
resolution.

topicality standard the
criterion used to resolve the
conflicts between competing
definitions.

traditional importance a
line of argument supporting
justification arguing that
some conventions of nations,
cultures, and communities
are valuable historically.

transition a word or phrase
that provides a logical bridge
from one argument to the
next, from one piece of
evidence to the next, or from
one argument to one piece of
evidence.

trivialization the process of
reducing the impact of a
specific argument in the
context of an entire debate.

turnaround an argument used
to answer a disadvantage or
value objection indicating
that affirming the resolution
actually diminishes the
disadvantage (link turn) or
indicating that the impact of
the argument is actually good
and not bad (impact turn).

U

unique describes the condition
of the countervalue when the
affirmative's defense of the
resolution alone bears a
relationship to the objection.

V

value an expression of the
worth of a person, process,
thing, or idea.

value context a standard that
uses specific circumstances
to assess the importance of
values.

value hierarchy *an argument that prioritizes values.*

value objection *an argument that indicates that competing values are more important than the value affirmed in the resolution.*

value translation *value criteria that seek to maximize one value through the implementation of another value that shares the* first value's ultimate objective.

value utility *a philosophical perspective that argues that the preferred value should be the one that provides the greatest good to the greatest number of people.*

voting issue *an argument that, independently of all other arguments in the debate, justifies voting for one side over the other.*

W

whole-resolution argument *an argument that suggests that the purpose of nonpolicy debate is to examine the probable truth or probable falsity of the general claim of the value resolution.*

Index